Eliminate the hassles  with others!

HAVE YOU EVER BEEN

- intimidated by persuasive salesmen or surly repairmen?
- reluctant to express your opinions in a group?
- concerned about being a disappointment in bed?
- nervous about making polite conversation?
- uncertain about asking someone for a date?
- afraid to talk back when you're treated unfairly?

If you have, it's time to get proven help from two noted psychologists—Doctors Alberti and Emmons of California Polytechnic State University, San Luis Obispo. Their revolutionary book "opens a whole new world of therapeutic interaction." —*Behavior Therapy*

"Interesting, readable and practical . . . provocative to both laymen and professional workers." —*Contemporary Psychology*

Stand Up, Speak Out, Talk Back!

by ROBERT E. ALBERTI, Ph.D.
and MICHAEL L. EMMONS, Ph.D.

PUBLISHED BY POCKET BOOKS NEW YORK

**POCKET BOOKS, a Simon & Schuster division of
GULF & WESTERN CORPORATION
1230 Avenue of the Americas, New York, N.Y. 10020**

Published by arrangement with Impact Publishers, Inc.

ISBN: 0-671-44207-4

First Pocket Books printing August, 1975

15   14   13   12

POCKET and colophon are trademarks of Simon & Schuster.

Printed in the U.S.A.

Acknowledgments

Since the first publication of *Your Perfect Right* in 1970, public and professional response to our program of assertive behavior training has been continuous and increasing. The expansion of knowledge and interest in this field has led to the development of *Stand Up, Speak Out, Talk Back!*, designed for a wide readership. We sincerely appreciate the vital contributions several persons have made to this book, and we acknowledge with thanks their dedicated efforts:

Special appreciation is due to Joseph Wolpe, who stimulated and encouraged our approach to assertive training.

Lachlan P. MacDonald has edited the manuscript and served as general consultant and agent on publication. In addition, his perceptiveness and creativity have contributed significantly to our theoretical conceptualization. He is also a valued personal friend.

Charles and Carita Merker, owner-operators of Grandview Printers, Glendale, Arizona, gave generously of their time and talents to help make possible the publication of the first edition of *Your Perfect Right*.

We appreciate the enthusiastic support and editorial judgment of Bernard W. Shir-Cliff, who aided us significantly in adapting material from *Your Perfect Right* for this new book.

Much recognition is due to our many professional

colleagues throughout the world who have contributed to our awareness of the values and the limitations of assertive behavior training through their research and clinical applications.

Deborah Alberti and Kay Emmons have been models of assertiveness, have encouraged, loved, and waited (not always quietly). Without them there would be no book. To them we dedicate this effort.

R.E.A.
M.L.E.

San Luis Obispo, California
May, 1975

We . . . were supposed to sit still, shut up, and take it in, conform, deny our experience and learn not to trust our own bodies or feelings of existence. Those ways are no longer adequate for me. So we are trying to give breath to those movements which exalt rather than put down the human, and which encourage persons to question in a positive way what human beings are and can become.

—John Vasconcellos in foreword to
Your Perfect Right, *second edition*

Table of Contents

I: TAKE CHARGE OF YOUR LIFE

II: THE ASSERTIVENESS TRAINING PROGRAM

III: BEYOND SELF-ASSERTION

I

Take Charge of Your Life

All men are born free and equal, and have certain natural, essential and unalienable rights.

—Constitution of Massachusetts, 1778

1

Human Rights and Personal Power

We write with an awareness of the sense of personal powerlessness felt by many people in our society today, living in crowded, noisy, polluted, unfriendly places where individuals count for little or nothing, where giant industries, or public utilities, or labor unions, or political establishments are in control. Despite an occasional Ralph Nader or John Gardner, the average citizen continues to feel controlled, exploited, and used by whoever finds in him/her a source of power or profit. The average citizen may feel that she/he is merely regarded as an expendable resource.

We don't agree. It is our conviction that the individual counts for more.

And that is the purpose of this book, to help overcome personal powerlessness, to help persons who feel somehow insignificant or frustrated in the total scheme of things. We do not simply blame this condition upon the modern technological world, but we do recognize that in such a world the need to reaffirm each other's individual value is of the highest priority.

The reader should understand that this is not a proposal for political, economic, or social revolution. We are here concerned with power on a much more personal level—at home, on the job, at school, in stores and restaurants, in club meetings, wherever the sense of personal insignificance or frustration is encountered.

We endorse without qualification the concept of the equality of human beings. Each individual has the same fundamental human rights as the other person in an interpersonal relationship, roles and titles notwithstanding. It is our goal to help more people to learn to exercise their perfect rights, without infringing upon the rights of others. On a broader scale, we hope you will become familiar with The Universal Declaration of Human Rights (Appendix).

We are greatly concerned about the strong tendency in our society to evaluate human beings on scales which make some persons "better" than others. Consider the following assumptions:

> Adults are better than children.
> Bosses are better than employees.
> Men are better than women.
> Whites are better than blacks.
> Physicians are better than plumbers.
> Teachers are better than students.
> Government officers are better than voters.
> Generals are better than privates.
> Winners are better than losers.

And so on, *ad infinitum.* Our social structures perpetuate these and similar myths, thereby allowing individual human beings in these roles to be treated as if they are of lesser value *as human beings,* rather than in the context of the hierarchy of roles.

In his foreword to the second edition of *Your Perfect Right,* John Vasconcellos, a member of the California Legislature, stated the context in which our approach to behavior can be best understood. He wrote:

> We are undergoing significant changes in every aspect of our society: religion, family, work, life

style, education and government. Many of our social institutions, through which people found security in the past, are no longer secure or present in the same way. Education, like society and all its other institutions, is experiencing painful and profound crisis and confusion.

I am aware that many persons continue to believe in a thrust towards betterment—call it evolutionary, intellectual, scientific or humanistic. It is vital that human beings, especially those with responsibility to and for others, attempt to make sense of what's happening—for their own fulfillment, and for that of others.

What we are going through now is the deepest and most dramatic of changes: how the human being views the human being, how man envisions himself as a person, what it means to be human, what consciousness means, what it means to have a body, to express emotions, and to relate authentically.

In traditional Western culture, man has been conditioned to see and experience himself in negative ways—with much fear and shame and guilt. Whatever the relationship (parent and child, teacher and student, priest and worshipper, politician and constituent), man was impressed to look outward and upward, to the authority figure, for instruction on how he ought to be.

Today this relationship is radically changing. Many persons are looking inward and envisioning personhood in a positive way. And when I radically change my self-concept (or better, self-esteem), then all social structures and relationships built upon self-denial, repression and authority come sharply into question. I challenge the assumption that someone else knows better than I do what's best for me. I question those institutions that tell me I need someone else to dictate to me how I ought to be. . . . Learning to be assertive is education for living, for being human, for becoming ourselves in much more human ways, and for making society more human too.

But finally, it is a matter of your own personal choice, and your own sense of yourself, and your own willingness to take the kinds of risks that make your own life personal, creative, meaningful and fulfilled.

Why This Book Was Written

Our analysis of the basic structures of Western society leads us to share John Vasconcellos' conclusion that assertive behavior is frequently squelched. The basic organization and teaching of families and of educational, business, and religious organizations have inhibited complete expression in interpersonal situations.

Women, children, and members of ethnic minorities in the United States have characteristically been taught that assertive behavior is the province of the white male adult. Indeed, such attitudes run deep and die hard in our culture.

It has been extremely difficult for the *haves* to acknowledge the human rights of the *have nots*. The gains resulting from the civil rights movement of the 1950's and 1960's were slow, painful, and tragically costly. In retrospect, one wonders if the changes are more than slight. The late President Lyndon Baines Johnson observed that the Civil Rights Acts of 1964, 1965, and 1968 were "the best bills we could get" from a Congress powerfully influenced by individuals who had dedicated their lives to the preservation of the *status quo ante*.

More recently, women have encountered similar resistance to their new efforts of self-assertion. Their husbands, their employers, their legislators, their President, have all demonstrated reluctance ranging from foot-dragging to open hostility and political battles. Yet women, too, are making overdue gains in recognition of their individual rights. We have noted an increase in assertive training workshops for women. The message is clear. Our cultural orientation to the development of appropriately assertive behavior has been inadequate. We must begin to value and reward the assertions of each individual, acknowledging his right to express himself without fear of guilt, valuing his right to an opinion, and recognizing his unique contribution.

In the family, individual rights are often promptly censored. Familiar admonitions are: "Don't you dare talk to your mother [father] that way!" "Children are to be seen, not heard." "Never let me hear you say that word again!" Obviously these common parental commands are not conducive to a child's assertion of self.

Teachers are especially guilty of anti-assertive behavior. Quiet, well-behaved children who do not question the system are rewarded, whereas those who buck the system in some way are dealt with sternly. It is an acknowledged conclusion among educators that the child's natural spontaneity in learning is "conditioned out" no later than the fourth or fifth grade.

The residue of parental and educational upbringing affects our functioning in our occupations and daily lives. Every employee is aware that typically one must not do or say anything that will "rock the boat" in an organization. The boss is "above" and others are "below" and feel obliged to go along with what is expected of them even if they consider the expectations completely inappropriate. Employees' early work experiences teach that if you "speak up" you are likely not to obtain a raise or recognition, and you may even lose your job. You quickly learn to be a "company person," to keep things running smoothly, to express few ideas of your own, to be careful how you act lest it "get back to the boss." The lesson is quite clear: in effect, be non-assertive in your work.

The teachings of contemporary churches seem to indicate that to be assertive in life is not the "religious" thing to do. Such qualities as humility, self-denial, and self-sacrifice are usually fostered to the exclusion of standing up for oneself. There is a mistaken notion that religious ideals of brotherhood must, in some esoteric way, be incompatible with feeling good about oneself and with being calm and confident in relationships with others. We believe that being assertive in life is in no way incongruent with the teachings of the major religious groups. If your escape from freedom-restricting behavior *allows* you to be of more service to your fellows as well as to yourself, what could be irreligious about that?

Political institutions, while not so likely as the home, school, and church to influence early development of assertive behavior, do little to encourage its expression by individual adults. Political decision-making has come only a short distance from the days of "star chambers," and it remains largely inaccessible to the average citizen. Nevertheless it is still true that the "squeaking wheel gets greased," and when individuals do become expressive enough, governments usually respond. It is our hope that more adequately assertive expression will preclude the necessity of aggressiveness among politically alienated activists.

It is common for a person who has been aggressive in a given situation to feel some guilt as a result of this behavior. It is less widely recognized that the assertive person also experiences such guilt as a result of childhood conditioning. The institutions of society have so carefully taught the inhibition of self-assertion that one may feel badly for defending even one's own reasonable rights.

It is not healthy to suffer guilt feelings for being one-self. Although families, schools, businesses, churches, and governments tend to deny self-assertion, we contend that *each person has the right to be and to express her/ himself, and to feel good (not guilty) about doing so, as long as she/he does not hurt others in the process.*

The anti-assertive influence of these basic societal systems has resulted in a "built-in" set of self-fulfilling limitations on the actions of many persons. Many people whose lives were constricted by an inability to be adequately assertive have achieved self-fulfillment by following the assertive training program of this book. You can too.

Who Will Read This Book?

This book is for all who wish to develop a more en-hancing personal existence on their own, and for those who will be instrumental in facilitating the personal growth of others. A book of broad appeal runs the risk of being "spread too thin;" however, we feel strongly that the concept of legitimate assertiveness is needed by many persons.

While this book is aimed at a general audience, we expect that many of the persons who read it will be en-gaged in, or training for, professional therapeutic or be-havior-modifying roles. Teachers, coaches, counselors, and personnel workers in schools and colleges find this book useful, as do those whose responsibilities are school-related, such as speech therapists. Professionals in private and agency therapeutic practice—psychia-trists, psychologists, medical doctors, marriage and fam-ily counselors, pastors, social workers, rehabilitation and employment counselors—find assertive training valuable in their practice. They also offer it as helpful reading for their clients. For some professionals this book provides a brief review and an organized approach to methods they already employ in varying degrees, and may serve to increase their effectiveness. Personnel and training officers in large industrial or government organizations are successfully utilizing the concepts and techniques described here. Also, this material has been applied by a wide variety of individuals engaged in work with community and youth organizations.

This book was written with practical application in mind and is organized to facilitate its usefulness in practice. The reader is urged to familiarize himself or herself with the concept of assertiveness, recognize its validity in one's own experience . . . and then *apply* its principles in personal life!

2

Are You in Charge of Your Own Life?

June and Paul have been married three years. Both have full-time jobs and they have agreed to share equally in household chores. In recent weeks June has realized that she is doing most of the housework. She has begun to feel resentment and hostility toward Paul. He seems unaware of any problem.

Ron has just been fired from his job. Although he is an effective and conscientious worker, Ron can't seem to control his temper at times. He goes along well for weeks, then suddenly blows up for no apparent reason. Today his boss asked him to stay overtime to finish an important assignment, and Ron flew into a rage.

Marilyn, on the other hand, can't seem to keep a secretary. In her busy advertising firm, Marilyn handles accounts for many large corporations and her clients feel she does an excellent job. Her staff, however, sees her very differently. The "queen bee" they call her— an office tyrant who runs her shop with an iron pen. Marilyn's "put-down" style of treating people has just resulted in another resignation.

June and Ron and Marilyn share a common problem. Each must learn to deal more effectively with life situations involving relationships with others. Can June act in her own best interest, stand up for herself without undue anxiety, and exercise her rights without denying Paul his? Can Ron learn to express himself more spontaneously, showing his anger in non-destructive ways at the moment when provocations occur, rather than bottling it up inside and eventually exploding (and losing his job)? As for Marilyn, although she usually gets her way, can she find a way to deal with her staff in mutual respect, maintaining her leadership without putting others down? Let's take a look at some of the possible alternatives for our three fictional characters.

June may continue to do Paul's share of the work, holding her true feelings inside until she develops migraine headaches or other physical symptoms, and reducing her own sense of self-worth. She might weakly hint around about the problem or assume indignantly that Paul should *know* how she feels. If her hostility builds up enough, she might start doing the housework with physical vengeance, slamming doors, banging furniture around. June could also pull the silent treatment, sulking or faking a sore back. We consider such behavior to be *non-assertive*. June is denying herself and not acting honestly or in accord with her own best interests. Ron's outbursts after "suffering in silence" are also a product of a non-assertive style.

At the other end of the scale is Marilyn's open hostility toward others. Her secretaries are confronted with Marilyn's attacking criticism several times a day. "Joan," she would scream, "can't you *ever* get those contracts in correct form? What the hell is wrong with you anyway?" She acts as if the only way to gain the respect and cooperation of her staff is to browbeat them into obedience. We have characterized this style of relating to others as *aggressive*. Although Marilyn gets her way, she does so at the expense of others, and in the process she loses their esteem.

It is our hope, of course, that neither the non-assertive nor the aggressive styles represent *your* way of dealing with others. A third alternative, an effective *assertive* response, is our preference, and in this book we will show you how to be an assertive person.

June, for example, could have responded assertively to the situation by sitting down with Paul at an appropriate time, and saying, "Paul, I've been quite upset about the 'balance of labor' around here recently, and I'd like to talk with you about it."

Paul would perhaps mumble, "Mm, hm."

June persists assertively, "You aren't honoring our agreement. Maybe we should hire someone to clean."

Paul is suddenly interested. "I didn't know you felt so strongly about it. I'd like to hire a housekeeper, but we can't afford it."

"That's true," responds June, "but I need for you to start helping again or for us to work out some other solution, since I can't do it all myself, nor should I have to."

Paul asks sincerely, "How can I help?"

Similar alternatives exist for Ron and Marilyn. Ron could develop the ability to react spontaneously to his boss's requests which upset him, rather than holding back until one request triggers the inevitable blowup. Dealing with situations assertively *as they occur* will prevent the need for that explosive confrontation which will probably cost Ron his job.

Marilyn's employees would work as hard (maybe harder) and respect her more if she treated them assertively with respect. No one likes to be humiliated, but everyone does make mistakes. She could have said, "Joan, you have not prepared these contracts correctly. They must be done over again." That statement, in a firm but non-hostile tone, would give the message clearly without attacking the secretary personally.

When a person develops an adequate repertoire of assertive behavior, she/he may choose an appropriate and self-fulfilling response in a variety of situations. One who is more able to be self-expressive and to do things on self-initiative reduces appreciably the former anxiety or tenseness in key situations, and enjoys an increase in her/his sense of worth as a person.

We submit that it is not only possible but most desirable that each of us develop a high sense of personal worth, and a behavioral style which is self-assertive. Neither self-denying nor other-denying behavior is good for you or the people around you. Let's look at the difference more closely.

In the *non-assertive* style, you are likely to hesitate, speak softly, look away, avoid the issue, agree regardless of your own feelings, not express opinions, value yourself "below" others, and hurt yourself to avoid any chance of hurting others.

In the *aggressive* style, you typically answer before the other person is through talking, speak loudly and abusively, glare at the other person, speak "past" the issue (accusing, blaming, demeaning), vehemently expound your feelings and opinions, value yourself "above" others, and hurt others to avoid hurting yourself.

In the *assertive* style, you will answer spontaneously, speak with a conversational tone and volume, look at the other person, speak to the issue, openly express your personal feelings and opinions (anger, love, disagreement, sorrow), value yourself equal to others, and hurt neither yourself nor others.

It is not difficult to see the advantage of the assertive response in countless interpersonal circumstances. We have devised an inventory of assertiveness so that you may check yourself. Be honest with yourself in answering these questions. This is not a "personality test;" it is merely a guide to help you assess your own self-assertiveness. We're not even going to give you a "magic formula" for scoring the inventory. How "well" you do depends upon your own standards. The real question is: How do *you* feel about the way you handle these situations?

1. Do you generally express what you feel?
2. Do you find it difficult to make decisions?
3. Are you openly critical of others' ideas, opinions, behavior?
4. Do you speak out in protest when someone takes your place in line?
5. Do you often avoid people or situations for fear of embarrassment?
6. Do you usually have confidence in your own judgment?
7. Do you insist that your spouse or roommate take on a fair share of household chores?
8. Are you prone to "fly off the handle"?
9. When a salesperson makes an effort, do you find it hard to say "No," even though the merchandise is not really what you want?
10. When a latecomer is waited on before you are, do you call attention to the situation?
11. Are you reluctant to speak up in a discussion or debate?
12. If a person has borrowed money (or a book, garment, thing of value) and is overdue in returning it, do you mention it?
13. Do you continue to pursue an argument after the other person has had enough?
14. When a person is highly unfair, do you say so?
15. Are you disturbed if someone watches you at work?

16. If someone keeps kicking or bumping your chair in a movie or a lecture, do you ask the person to stop?

17. Do you find it difficult to maintain eye contact when talking to another person?

18. In a good restaurant, when your meal is improperly prepared or served, do you ask the waiter/waitress to correct the situation?

19. When you discover merchandise is faulty, do you return it for an adjustment?

20. Do you show your anger by name-calling or obscenities?

21. Do you try to be a wallflower or a piece of the furniture in social situations?

22. Do you insist that your landlord (mechanic, repairman, etc.) make repairs, adjustments or replacements which are his responsibility?

23. Do you often step in and make decisions for others?

24. Are you able openly to express love and affection?

25. Are you able to ask your friends for small favors or help?

26. Do you think you always have the right answer?

27. When you differ with a person you respect, are you able to speak up for your own viewpoint?

28. Are you able to refuse unreasonable requests made by friends?

29. Do you have difficulty complimenting or praising others?

30. If you are disturbed by someone smoking near you, can you say so?

31. Do you shout or use bullying tactics to get others to do as you wish?

32. Do you finish other people's sentences for them?

33. Do you get into physical fights with others, especially with strangers?

34. At family meals, do you control the conversation?

35. When you meet a stranger, are you the first to introduce yourself and begin a conversation?

The key to this inventory is *choice*. There is no single way that one *must* act in a particular situation. We hope you can *choose* for yourself how you will act, and not be manipulated by circumstances or people.

If your answers to the inventory suggest that you *are* often "pushed around" in such situations, you are far from alone. Recent research has shown that as many as *eighty per cent* of us will comply with an unreasonable request without objecting! People emptied their pockets for a stranger who suggested they may have inadvertently picked up his ring in a telephone booth. Only one in five refused. A similar percentage remained silent while rock music was played at high volume by one member of a group while other members were attempting to complete a written test. Many (most?) people evidently are willing to allow themselves to be victims of such "little murders."

But it doesn't have to be that way! We have found that almost anyone can learn to be consistently more assertive, and thereby enhance feelings of self-worth. By learning to deal with conflicts as they arise, you do not allow the feelings of anger, frustration, or guilt to build up, as Ron did, until you "explode."

"Well," you say, "that's all fine for those people who *are* assertive, but I'm not. I just can't express myself that way. I never know what to say." On the contrary, *you can!* There aren't any "naturally" assertive persons, only those who have learned to behave as they do. And it's never too late for you to begin the same process.

3

How Do You Feel About Yourself?

What have you done *for yourself* recently? Have you spent time or money on *you?* Tried a new hobby? Tasted a new food? Bought something you wanted "on impulse"? Designed or built something on your own?

Take some time now to take stock of your feelings toward yourself—and what you do about them. Keep in mind that *saying* you like yourself means little if you are *doing* nothing for yourself!

Dr. Alberti has developed the following brief inventory of "taking-care-of-yourself" behavior. Use it to check up on yourself. There are no correct answers, but the results should give you an idea of how much value you really place on *you!*

A Behavioral Model for Personal Growth

Psychologist Carl Rogers, in his important book *On Becoming a Person,* has identified three major characteristics of personal growth within a humanistic framework which lend themselves readily to translation into specific behaviors. We can use the following checklists as a "model" for this process of identifying specific acts involved in each of Rogers' dimensions of growth.

Increasing Openness to Experience

How recently have you

- ... participated in a new sport or game?
- ... changed your views on an important (political, personal, professional) issue?
- ... tried a new hobby or craft?
- ... taken a course in a new field?
- ... studied a new language or culture?
- ... spent fifteen minutes or more paying attention to your body feelings, senses (relaxation, tension, sensuality)?
- ... listened for fifteen minutes or more to a religious, political, professional, or personal viewpoint with which you disagreed?
- ... tasted a new food, smelled a new odor, listened to a new sound?
- ... allowed yourself to cry? or to say "I care about you"? or to laugh until you cried? or to scream at the top of your lung capacity? or to admit you were afraid?
- ... watched the sun (or moon) rise or set? or a bird soar on the wind's currents? or a flower open to the sun?
- ... traveled to a place you had never been before?
- ... spent an hour or more really communicating (actively listening and responding honestly) with a person of a different cultural or racial background?
- ... taken a "fantasy trip"—allowing your imagination to run freely for ten minutes to an hour or more?

Increasing Existential Living

How recently have you

   ... done something you felt like doing at that moment, without regard for the consequences?

   ... stopped to "listen" to what was going on inside you, really concentrating your awareness on what was happening within you at that moment?

   ... spontaneously expressed a feeling—anger, joy, fear, sadness, caring—without "thinking about it"?

   ... done what you wanted to do, instead of what you thought you "should" do?

   ... allowed yourself to spend time or money on an immediate "payoff" rather than saving for tomorrow?

   ... bought something you wanted "on impulse"?

   ... done something no one (including you) expected you to do?

Increasing Trust in One's Organism

How recently have you

   ... done what "felt right" to you, against the advice of others?

   ... allowed yourself to experiment creatively with a new approach to an old problem?

   ... expressed an unpopular opinion assertively in the face of majority opposition?

   ... used your own intellectual reasoning ability to work out a solution to a difficult problem?

   ... made a decision and acted upon it right away?

... acknowledged by your actions that you can direct your own life (refuse an unreasonable request, not "ask permission" to do what you want)?

... cared enough about yourself to get a physical exam (within a year)?

... told others of your religious faith, or philosophy of life?

... assumed a position of leadership in your community, or an organization, or your profession?

... asserted your feelings when you were treated unfairly?

... risked sharing your personal feelings with another person?

... designed and/or built something on your own?

... admitted you were wrong?

... admitted you were right?

The way people answer these questions says a good deal about how they see themselves. We hope you are pleased with the results of your self-check. If not, the inventory may suggest some areas where you could begin to take better care of yourself. If you *like* yourself, if you value yourself as a person, if you have what psychologists call "a good self-concept," you very likely found that you regularly do many of the things listed above. You are actively engaged in life, finding out about new people, places, and things, savoring each hour, acting spontaneously, trusting your own judgment, sharing yourself with others.

Poor Self-Concept

Unfortunately, many individuals find it really difficult to care for themselves. The person with a "poor self-concept" not only *believes* that he/she is worth less than most other folks, this person *acts* accordingly. Thus, his/her responses to the checklist would point out self-defeating behavior: seldom really enjoying daily activities, almost never seeking out new experiences or people, just "getting by," fearful of depending on one's own judgment or trusting oneself.

Behavior which enables a person to act in his/her own best interests, to stand up for her/himself without undue anxiety, to express honest feelings comfortably, or to exercise her/his own rights without denying the rights of others we call *assertive behavior*. By contrast, the non-assertive person is likely to think of the appropriate response after the opportunity has passed. At the other extreme, an *aggressive* person may respond too vigorously, making a deep and negative impression, and may later be sorry for it. It is our purpose in this book to assist you to develop a more adequate repertoire of assertive behavior, to help you to be able to choose from among appropriate and self-fulfilling responses in a variety of situations.

Commonly, people mistake aggression for assertion, but the assertive individual does not malign others or deny their rights, running roughshod over people. The assertive person is open and flexible, genuinely concerned with the rights of others, as well as with self.

Research has shown conclusively that a person who becomes more able to stand up for her/himself and to take individual initiative reduces appreciably anxiety or tenseness in key situations, and increases his/her sense of worth as a person. This same sense of worth is often lacking in the aggressive person, whose aggressiveness may mask self-doubts and guilt. Individuals who have developed greater assertiveness through the procedures described in this book also have shown significant gains in self-acceptance and decreases in anxiety.

Two years ago, as a "successful" aerospace executive (with $40,000-plus income, big house, busy social calendar, etc.), Ken celebrated his fortieth birthday—and conducted a major evaluation of his life. He noted that he was usually tired, seldom really saw his family, gained little enjoyment from the superficial parties he attended, and was enjoying *almost none* of the leisure activities he fantasized for himself. In short, although apparently effective as an executive, Ken was not at all in charge of his own life! Moreover, he was very unhappy. Having thus examined his life and realized how little he had done for himself, Ken allowed himself to trust his own good sense. He quit his job, sold the too-big house, and realized a boyhood dream by becoming owner-manager of a small hardware store. Now he keeps short business hours, doesn't fly to Washington or Florida, spends time caring for himself and his family, and has discovered that he *likes himself* much better! He is now doing for himself what feels right to him, and his life is much more rewarding.

If you go through life inhibited, giving in to the wishes of others, holding your own desires inside yourself, or conversely, destroying others in order to have your way, your feeling of personal worth will be low. Even such bodily complaints as headaches, general fatigue, stomach disturbances, rashes, and asthma are often the result of failure to develop assertive behavior. The assertive individual is fully in charge of her/himself in interpersonal relationships, feels confident and capable without cockiness or hostility, is basically spontaneous in the expression of feelings and emotions, and is generally looked up to by others.

The professional "rat race" is of course only one area in which we allow our lives to be out of our own control. Ken was fortunate in having the *awareness* of his dissatisfaction, the *trust* in himself to act on it, and some financial *resources* to facilitate the change. Many of us lack one or more of Ken's fortuitous combination. But "good fortune" and "pure luck" are not the same thing! You can make your own good fortune. If you are aware of a needed change, and willing to trust your own capacities, you can very likely develop the resources to make it possible. Our first book, for example, was the product of our desire to have our message read, our willingness to believe we could do it, and the investment of about $300 each in our own "publishing business"—which eventually (at this writing) grew into over 65,000 copies of the book (that first $600 bought us 1,000 copies), another book, a newsletter, and the recognition of our publisher, Pocket Books, which resulted in the pages you are reading.

4

Assertive, Non-Assertive, and Aggressive Behavior

Janet is 23, attractive, single, and about to complete a program of management training in a large industrial organization. Despite her professional effectiveness, Janet finds it difficult to say "no" in some circumstances. Fred, whom she has known at work for several months, has asked her out repeatedly. She did accept once, and found him to be not only too sexually aggressive, but also uninteresting. She has since offered a variety of excuses—a new one for each refusal ("I have to set my hair," "I have a date," "I have a report to complete." . . .). He has just asked her out again. Janet might reply:

(1) "Uh . . . well . . . I have to go to a meeting that evening . . . with some friends . . . it's important . . . uh . . ."

(2) "Look, how many times do I have to turn you down before you get the idea? Get off my back! I'll let you know if I want to go out with you, but don't hold your breath!"

(3) "I don't want to hurt your feelings, but it would be unfair of me to accept. I really don't want to go out with you and it's better that I let you know honestly."

Clearly, the (1) and (2) responses are inadequate. With (2), Janet shows little sensitivity to Fred's feelings and uses aggressive language to put him off. In contrast, she denies herself in sample (1), again using the

36

"excuse" technique, which is dishonest, not really expressive of her feelings, and denies Fred what might have been the first honest feedback he's had ("his best friends won't tell him!"). Janet can save herself and Fred considerable hurt and awkwardness by using (3), a straightforward, assertive response.

Our Western way of life cultivates conflicting ways of behaving in many interpersonal areas. A typical example is found in the common attitudes and teachings about human sexuality. Sexual restraint is the societal norm of the American middle-class family, school and church. The popular media, however, virtually bombard audiences with a different view of sexuality. On one hand, Janet is expected to be sweet and innocently non-assertive, whereas on the other she is rewarded for being sultry, vampish and sensual. Sexual aggressiveness, especially in the male, is highly valued; the lover is glorified in print and on the screen, and admired by his peers. Paradoxically, he is cautioned to date "respectable" girls and warned that sexual intercourse is guiltless only after marriage. In addition to the personal conflicts resulting from such teaching, stereotypic male/female role behavior is emphasized, perpetuating "double standards" and distorted notions about "manhood" and "womanhood."

Further examples of conflicts between "recommended" and "rewarded" behavior are evident. Even though it is typically understood that one should respect the rights of others, all too often we observe that parents, teachers and churches contradict these values by their own actions. Tact, diplomacy, politeness, refined manners, modesty, and self-denial are generally praised, yet to "get ahead" it is often acceptable to "step on" others.

The male child is carefully coached to be strong, brave, and dominant. His aggressiveness is condoned and accepted, as in the pride felt by a father whose son is in trouble for busting the neighborhood bully in the nose. Ironically (and a source of much confusion for the child), the same father will likely encourage his son to "have respect for his elders," "let others go first," "be polite."

Although it is seldom openly admitted, the athlete who participates in competitive sports knows that if he or she has been aggressive or perhaps "bent" the rules a little, it is acceptable because "what's important is not how you play the game, but whether or not you win." (The physical fitness purist who would argue with this statement is invited to contrast the rewards for winning coaches with those for losing coaches who "build character.") Woody Hayes, much acclaimed football coach at Ohio State University, is quoted as saying, "Show me a good loser, and I'll show you a loser."

We believe that you should be able to *choose for yourself* how you will act in a given circumstance. If your "polite restraint" response is too well developed, you may be unable to make the choice to act as you would like to. If your aggressive response is over-developed, you may be unable to achieve your own goals without hurting others. This freedom of choice and exercise of self-control is possible when you develop assertive responses for situations in which you have previously acted non-assertively or aggressively because of anxiety.

In Chapter 2, we defined assertive, non-assertive, and aggressive behavior. Further examples contrasting assertive with non-assertive and aggressive actions will help to clarify these concepts. The pattern which appears in the following chart is also demonstrated in each of the examples which follow. The chart displays several feelings and consequences typical for the person (actor) whose behavior is non-assertive, assertive, or aggressive. Also shown, for each of these modes of behavior, are the likely consequences for the person toward whom the action is directed (acted upon).

It may be seen in the chart that in the case of a *non-assertive* response in a given situation, the actor is typically denying self, and is inhibited from expressing his actual feelings. Often hurt and anxious as a result of this inadequate behavior, allowing others to choose for him, he seldom achieves his own desired goals.

The person who carries a desire for self-expression to the extreme of *aggressive* behavior accomplishes life goals usually at the expense of others. Although frequently finding this behavior self-enhancing and expressive of feelings in the situation, she/he usually hurts others in the process by making choices for them, and by minimizing their worth as persons.

NON-ASSERTIVE BEHAVIOR	AGGRESSIVE BEHAVIOR	ASSERTIVE BEHAVIOR
As Actor	*As Actor*	*As Actor*
Self-denying	Self-enhancing at expense of another	Self-enhancing
Inhibited	Expressive	Expressive
Hurt, anxious	Depreciates others	Feels good about self
Allows others to choose	Chooses for others	Chooses for self
Does not achieve desired goal	Achieves desired goal by hurting others	May achieve desired goal
As Acted Upon	*As Acted Upon*	*As Acted Upon*
Guilty or angry	Self-denying	Self-enhancing
Depreciates actor	Hurt, defensive, humiliating	Expressive
Achieves desired goal at actor's expense	Does not achieve desired goal	May achieve desired goal

Aggressive behavior commonly results in a "put-down" of the recipient. His/her rights have been denied, and she/he feels hurt, defensive, and humiliated. His/her goals in the situation, of course, are not achieved. Although the aggressive person may achieve his/her goal, she/he may also generate hatred and frustration, which may later reappear as vengeance.

In contrast, appropriately *assertive* behavior in the same situation would be self-enhancing for the actor, and an honest expression of feelings, usually achieving his/her goals, having chosen for self how she/he will act. A good feeling about self typically accompanies the assertive response.

Similarly, when the consequences of these three contrasting behaviors are viewed from the perspective of the person "acted upon" (i.e., the individual toward whom the behavior is directed) a parallel pattern emerges. Non-assertive behavior often produces feelings ranging from sympathy to outright contempt toward the actor. Also, the person acted upon may feel guilt or anger at having achieved her/his own goals at the actor's expense. In contrast, a transaction involving assertion enhances feelings of self-worth and permits full expression of self. In addition, while the actor achieves *his/her* goals, the goals of the individual acted upon may also be achieved.

In summary, then, it is clear that the actor is hurt by self-denial in non-assertive behavior; the person(s) toward whom she/he acts may be hurt in aggressive behavior. In the case of assertion, neither person is hurt, and unless their goal achievement is mutually exclusive, both may succeed.

This pattern is most easily seen through examples of each of these three types of behavior—non-assertive, aggressive, assertive—in some life situations. Let's examine several such situations, most of which are common to everyone's experience. Some are even more dramatic demonstrations of the negative effects in the lives of some people from non-assertive or aggressive behavior.

Read each situation carefully, then pause for a moment and consider your own most likely response before you go on to read the three sample responses. There could be, of course, as many different possible responses as there are people! We have shown three merely to simplify illustration of the differences among the types. At the conclusion of the chapter, we have offered a few additional comments about the typical patterns of non-assertive, assertive, and aggressive behavior.

"DINING OUT"

Mr. and Mrs. A are at dinner in a moderately expensive restaurant. Mr. A has ordered a rare steak, but when the steak is served, Mr. A finds it to be very well done, contrary to his order. His behavior is:

Non-assertive: Mr. A grumbles to his wife about the "burned" meat, and observes that he won't patronize this restaurant in the future. He says nothing to the waitress, responding "Fine!" to her inquiry "Is everything all right?" His dinner and evening are highly unsatisfactory, and he feels guilty for having taken no action. Mr. A's estimate of himself and Mrs. A's estimate of him are both deflated by the experience.

Aggressive: Mr. A angrily summons the waitress to his table. He berates her loudly and unfairly for not complying with his order. His actions ridicule the waitress and embarrass Mrs. A. He demands and receives another steak, this one more to his liking. He feels in control of the situation, but Mrs. A's embarrassment creates friction between them, and spoils their evening. The waitress is humiliated and angry and loses her poise for the rest of the evening.

Assertive: Mr. A motions the waitress to his table. Noting that he had ordered a rare steak, he shows her the well-done meat, asking politely but firmly that it be returned to the kitchen and replaced with the rare-cooked steak he originally requested. The waitress apologizes for the error, and shortly returns with a rare steak. The A's enjoy dinner, tip accordingly, and Mr. A feels satisfaction with himself. The waitress is pleased with a satisfied customer and an adequate tip.

"SOMETHING BORROWED"

Helen is a college sophomore, bright, attractive, a good student liked by teachers and peers. She lives in a residence hall with two roommates in a suite arrangement with six other girls. All of the girls date quite regularly. One evening, as Helen's roommates are dressing for their dates (Helen plans a quiet evening working on a term paper), Mary says that she is going out with a "really special" young man, and hopes to make a good impression. She asks Helen if she may borrow and wear a new and quite expensive necklace Helen has just received from her brother, who is overseas in military service. Helen and her brother are very close, and the necklace means a great deal to her. Her response is:

Non-assertive: She swallows her anxiety about loss or damage to the necklace, her feeling that its special meaning makes it too personal to lend, and says, "Sure!" She denies herself, reinforces Mary for making an unreasonable request, and worries all evening (which makes little contribution to the term paper).

Aggressive: Helen shows her outrage at her friend's request, tells her "absolutely not," and proceeds to upbraid her severely for even daring to ask "such a stupid question." She humiliates Mary and generally makes a fool of herself. Later she feels uncomfortable and guilty, and this interferes with her work on the paper. Mary's hurt feelings are carried into her date, and she has a miserable time, puzzling and dismaying the young man. Thereafter the relationship between Helen and Mary becomes very strained.

Assertive: She explains the significance of the necklace to her roommate, and politely but firmly observes that the request is an unreasonable one since this piece of jewelry is particularly personal. She later feels good for having asserted herself, and Mary, recognizing the validity of Helen's response, makes a big hit with the young man by being more honestly herself.

" 'HAVE A JOINT' "

Pam is a friendly, outgoing secretary who has been dating an attractive young man for whom she cares a great deal. One evening he invites her to attend a small get-together with two other couples, both of whom are married. As all become acquainted at the party, Pam is enjoying herself. After an hour or so, one of the married men brings out several cigarettes which he identifies as marijuana and suggests that they all smoke. Everyone eagerly joins in except Pam, who does not wish to experiment with marijuana. She is in conflict because the boy she admires is smoking marijuana and as he offers her a cigarette she decides to be:

Non-assertive: She accepts the marijuana and pretends to have smoked it before. She carefully watches the others to see how they smoke. Inside, she dreads the possibility that they may ask her to smoke more. Others are speaking of getting "stoned" and Pam is worried about what her friend is thinking about her.

She has denied herself, been dishonest with her boy-friend, and feels remorseful for giving in to something she did not wish to do.

Aggressive: Pam is visibly upset when offered the marijuana and blasts the young man for bringing her to a party of this "low type." She states that she wants to be taken home right away rather than stay with such people. When the others at the party say that she does not have to smoke if she doesn't wish to, she is not appeased and continues to be quite indignant. Her friend is humiliated, embarrassed before his friends, and disappointed in her. Although he remains cordial toward Pam as he takes her home, he does not offer an invitation for a future date.

Assertive: Pam does not accept the cigarette, replying simply, "No, thank you. I don't care for one." She goes on to explain that she hasn't smoked pot before and doesn't wish to. She expresses her preference that the others not smoke, but acknowledges their right to make their own choices.

"THE HEAVYWEIGHT"

Mr. and Mrs. B, who have been married nine years, have been having marital problems recently because he insists that she is overweight and needs to reduce. He brings the subject up continually, pointing out that she is no longer the girl he married (who was 25 pounds lighter), that such overweight is bad for her health, that she is a bad example for the children, and so on.

In addition, he teases her about being "chunky," looks longingly at thin girls, commenting how attractive they look, and makes references to her figure in front of their friends. Mr. B has been reacting this way for the past three months and Mrs. B is highly upset. She has been attempting to lose weight for those three months but with little success. Following Mr. B's most recent rash of criticism, Mrs. B is:

Non-assertive: She apologizes for her weight, makes feeble excuses or simply doesn't reply to some of Mr. B's comments. Internally, she feels both hostile toward her husband for his nagging, and guilty about being overweight. Her feelings of anxiety make it even more difficult for her to lose weight and the battle continues.

Aggressive: Mrs. B goes into a long tirade about how her husband isn't any great bargain any more either! She brings up the fact that at night he falls asleep on the couch half the time, and that he is a lousy sex partner and doesn't pay sufficient attention to her. None of these comments are pertinent to the issue at hand, but Mrs. B continues. She complains that he humiliates her in front of the children and their close friends and acts like "a lecherous old man" by the way he eyes the sexy girls. In her anger she succeeds only in wounding Mr. B and driving a wedge between them by "defending" herself with a counterattack on him.

Assertive: Approaching her husband when they are alone and will not be interrupted, Mrs. B indicates that she feels that Mr. B is correct about her need to lose weight, but she does not care for the way he keeps after her about the problem or the manner in which he does so. She points out that she is doing her best and is having a difficult time losing the weight and maintaining the loss. He acknowledges the ineffectiveness of his harping, and they work out together a plan in which he will systematically reinforce her for her efforts to lose weight.

"THE NEIGHBORHOOD KID"

Mr. and Mrs. E have a boy two years old and a baby girl two months old. Over the last several nights their neighbor's son, who is 17, has been sitting in his own driveway in his car with his stereo tape player blaring loudly. He begins just about the time the E's two young children retire in their bedroom on the side of the house where the boy plays the music. The loud music awakens the children each night and it has been impossible for the E's to get the children to bed until the music stops. Mr. and Mrs. E are both disturbed and decide to be:

Non-assertive: Mr. and Mrs. E move the children into their own bedroom on the other side of the house, wait until the music stops around 1 A.M., then transfer the children back to their own rooms. Then they go to bed much past their own usual bedtime. They continue to quietly curse the teenager and soon become alienated from their neighbors.

Aggressive: Mr. and Mrs. E call the police and protest that "one of those wild teenagers" next door is creating a disturbance. They demand that the police "do their duty" and stop the noise at once. The police do talk with the boy and his parents, who become very upset and angry as a result of their embarrassment about the police visit. They denounce the E's tactics in reporting to the police without speaking to them first, and resolve to avoid further association with them.

Assertive: Both Mr. and Mrs. E go over to the boy's house and indicate to him that his stereo is keeping the children awake at night. They ask what arrangement they could work out concerning the music so that it would not disturb their children's sleep. The boy is reluctantly agreeable to setting a lower volume during the late hours, but appreciates the E's cooperative attitude. Both parties feel good about the outcome.

" 'I'VE HAD IT!' "

Mark, 28, came home today to find a note from his wife saying that she has initiated divorce proceedings. He is emotionally upset by her action, especially since she did not tell him face to face. As he attempts to control himself and understand why she reacted this way, he rereads her note: "Mark, we have been married for three whole years and you have never for one instant let me stand up for myself and act like a human being. You constantly tell me what to do, and *you* make all of the decisions! You will never learn to show tenderness and warmth toward anyone. I dread having children for fear they will be treated as I am. I have learned to lose all respect and admiration for you. Last night when you beat me was the final straw. I am divorcing you." Mark decides to react to her note by being:

Non-assertive: He feels all alone, sorry for himself and yet remorseful. He begins drinking and finally gets up enough nerve to call his wife at her parents' home. On the phone he pleads for her forgiveness, asking her to return, promising he will reform.

Aggressive: Mark becomes violently angry at his wife's behavior and seeks her out. He roughly grabs her arm and demands that she come home where she belongs. He indicates that she is his wife and *must* do what he says. She struggles and resists, and her parents intervene and call the police.

Assertive: Mark phones his wife indicating that he realizes it is basically his fault, but that he would like to change. He tells of his willingness to make an appointment with a marriage counselor and is hopeful that she will attend with him.

"THE LOSER"

Russell is a 22-year-old school dropout who works in a plastics factory. He lives alone in a small one-room walk-up apartment. Russell has had no dates for the past fourteen months. He left school after a series of depressing events—academic failures, a "Dear John" letter, and some painful harassment by other students. He has been in jail overnight for drunkenness on two recent occasions. Yesterday he received a letter from his mother, inquiring about his well-being, but primarily devoted to a discussion of his brother's recent successes. Today his supervisor berated him harshly and somewhat unjustly for a mistake which was actually the supervisor's own responsibility. In addition, a secretary in the plant turned down his invitation to dinner. When he arrived at his apartment that evening. feeling particularly depressed and overwrought, his landlord met him at the door with a tirade about "drunken bums" and a demand (one week early) that this month's rent be paid on time. Russell's response is:

Non-assertive: He takes on himself the burden of the landlord's attack, feeling added guilt and even greater depression. A sense of helplessness overcomes him. He wonders how his brother can be so successful while he himself seems so worthless. The secretary's rejection and the boss's criticism strengthen his conviction that he is "no damn good." Deciding the world would be a better place without him, he finds the small revolver he has been hiding in his room, and begins loading it for the purpose of committing suicide.

Aggressive: The landlord has added the final straw to Russell's burden. He becomes extremely angry and pushes the landlord out of the way. Once alone in his room, he resolves to "get" the people who have been making his life so miserable recently—the supervisor, the secretary, the landlord, and possibly others as well. He finds his revolver and begins loading it, with the intent of going out after dark to shoot the people who have hurt him.

Assertive: Russell responds firmly to the landlord, noting that he has paid his rent regularly and that it is not due for another week. He reminds the landlord of a broken rail on the stairway and the plumbing repairs which were to have been accomplished weeks earlier. The following morning, after giving his life situation a great deal of thought, Russell calls the local mental health clinic to ask for help. At work he approaches the supervisor calmly and explains the circumstances surrounding the mistake. Though somewhat defensive, the supervisor acknowledges his error and apologizes for his aggressive behavior.

"DOOR-TO-DOOR SALESMAN"

Jack, a college senior who will graduate this June, is busily completing his last courses and submitting his independent study project to his adviser. Jack is married to Carolyn, who is a graduate student at the same university. During the past week, insurance companies have begun to call Jack and Carolyn to offer the "Grad Man Plan," "Super Security," and the "Lifeline"— "special" insurance programs designed for college graduates. Carolyn and Jack have decided not to purchase any insurance until both have completed their degree programs. After dinner one evening, a personable young man appears at the door and announces that he has the "Top Dog Plan." Jack is:

Non-assertive: He invites the young man in and agrees to listen to his presentation, "although I'm not really in the market for insurance."

Aggressive: He says, in a loud, angry voice: "You damn insurance people are hounding us to death. You're the fourth one this week, and I'm fed up with all these intrusions. Get the hell out of here and tell your buddies that I'll shoot the next S.O.B. who comes around to sell me insurance!"

Assertive: He says, in a conversational, firm voice: "No. I'm not interested in any insurance. Good night."

"TIME TO RETIRE"

Mrs. K, a retired widow who lives in Senior City, is a creative, independent person, who enjoys working in her garden and painting a good deal more than she does gossiping with her neighbors. Her watercolors, in fact, have won numerous awards, and are sufficiently marketable to earn a sizable portion of Mrs. K's income.

A neighbor, Ms. R, "drops in for a chat" two or three times a week. Usually Mrs. K enjoys these visits, but in the past month they have occurred almost daily, and she has become somewhat annoyed. Moreover, the loss of time has begun to interfere with her painting—which could have direct economic consequences. Still, she doesn't want to hurt her friend's feelings. As she opens the door and finds Ms. R, she chooses to be:

Non-assertive: She smiles broadly and says, "Oh hello, R. I wondered if you might be coming over today! Please come in and have some coffee . . . though I'm, uh . . . pretty busy . . ."

Aggressive: Her expression becomes angry as she says, "R, are you here again? It's the third time this week! How can I get any work done when you're hanging around all the time? Why don't you call before you come over? Don't you have a home of your own?"

Assertive: She smiles but remains firm, saying, "Oh,

R, I just can't visit today. We've spent a good deal of time talking this week, and although I've enjoyed it, I just can't afford any more. I must get some painting done today. In fact, I'd like to set up a sort of 'limit' on our visits—I can get carried away and I do need to discipline myself to work!"

By now, you no doubt have the idea! Obviously there are many possible responses to each of the situations we have considered. In some of the examples, the response that came to mind for yourself was probably quite different from all three of our alternatives. Nevertheless these common styles people use in handling such life situations help to clarify the nature of assertiveness.

The most effective method of determining the adequacy of your own assertiveness is simply to listen honestly to yourself as you describe your relationships with others who are important to you. Depending upon age and lifestyle, make a careful examination of your interactions with parents, peers, co-workers, classmates, spouse, children, bosses, employees, teachers, salesmen, neighbors, and relatives. Who is dominant in these specific relationships? Are you easily taken advantage of in dealing with others? Do you express your feelings and ideas openly in most circumstances? Do you take advantage of and/or hurt others frequently?

Your honest responses to such questions can provide hints which may lead you to explore in greater depth your assertive, non-assertive, or aggressive behavior. We think you will find such self-examination rewarding, and a very important step on your journey toward increased interpersonal effectiveness.

5

"But I Am Assertive . . . Sometimes!"

Should one be assertive all the time? Is there only one "correct" way to handle situations? How about the differences in people?

As we look back over Chapter 4 and the array of examples there, a few general ideas begin to emerge:

(1) It is possible to express oneself assertively without hurting the other person in the process. Once again, this is the *definition* of assertive behavior: self-expression without stepping on others. Janet's would-be friend was no doubt disappointed when she refused his invitation—but by acting assertively, she was able to free herself from his attentions without crushing his self-esteem. Ms. R could more readily accept Mrs. K's request for time alone as long as she knows it is based on her friend's needs and is not a personal rejection.

(2) Such assertions will usually accomplish your goal. Not always, of course; life offers no guarantees. Yet hundreds of people have told us how they· are amazed by how responsive people are to simple assertions. All of the heart pounding and self-doubt fly out the window when the response is "Sure! I didn't realize I was bothering anybody. Sorry!" or "I'll be glad to help!" or "I only wish you had told me sooner so we could have taken care of the problem before! Thanks for letting me know!"

(3) Everyone is sometimes non-assertive, sometimes aggressive, and sometimes assertive—and that is okay! We all act in each of these ways at times. The problems arise when we are non-assertive or aggressive too often for our own good! And when we are no longer making the choices for ourselves.

We are not expecting you to become assertive all the time. There is no "right" way to handle all situations, no "magic formula" that will make everything fall into place. Don't waste your time and energy. The search is futile, and if you are seeking that sort of answer to life, we can't be of much help.

Instead, our efforts are directed toward giving you choices in life. We believe that if you truly are assertive *when you want to be,* that's all you or we could ask for. We have found that for too many folks, unfortunately, such a choice is not available. They are controlled by habits, by other people, by situations, and are unable to choose for themselves how they will act. Consider Jane, who felt it necessary to ask her husband if she could kiss him or sit on his lap!

For many people, such inhibitions are *situational;* that is, they have difficulty expressing themselves (or aggressively come on too strong) only in particular circumstances. Jane, for example, may be perfectly comfortable dealing with others in a business office—perhaps she is simply intimidated by her husband. We often see persons, however, who are *generally* living a non-assertive or aggressive life. They are controlled or controlling in almost all of their dealings with others, and are making few real choices about how they will act. Let's look at them in more detail.

General and Situational Non-Assertiveness

Sir Winston Churchill once said, "An appeaser is one who feeds a crocodile hoping it will eat him last." Two concepts of non-assertiveness are useful as we consider how to develop more adaptive responses to life situations which call for assertiveness. The first concerns those individuals whose behavior is typically adequate and self-enhancing; however, *certain situations* stimulate a great deal of anxiety in them which prevents fully adequate responses to that particular situation. We identify this category as *situational non-assertiveness*.

The second category, *generalized non-assertiveness*, includes those persons whose behavior is typically non-assertive. This individual, often observed as shy, timid, or reserved, finds himself unable to assert rights or act on feelings under *most or nearly all circumstances*. She/he will not do anything to disturb anyone. She/he is constantly giving in to any request received or else feels guilty for turning someone down. She/he has always done what Mom and Dad wanted, with no ideas of independent value. Whereas most persons will at least protest a little when their rights are badly abused, the general non-asserter, cowed by others, will say nothing at all. For example, if others are making undue noise and interfering with one's enjoyment of a performance, most of us will, when sufficiently provoked, ask them to respect our desire for quiet, whereas the generally non-assertive person will suffer in silence. She/he may even be self-accusatory: "I must be selfish and unfriendly to think that the other person is wrong." It is not unusual for this person to go out of his/her way to let others take advantage. Some general non-asserters ask permission to do what most people regard as their perfect right. Harry let someone borrow his car, supposedly for the day. When, three days later, the person returned the car with the gas tank almost empty and no explanation whatever as to what had happened, Harry said nothing—although his head was in a "fog" and his stomach in turmoil.

The generally non-assertive person, therefore, is one who finds his/her own self-esteem very low, and for whom very uncomfortable anxiety is generated by nearly all social situations. The feelings of inadequacy, lack of acknowledgment of one's own self-worth, and the physical discomfort induced by generalized anxiety may call for in-depth treatment. The extreme inhibition and lack of emotional responsiveness of this non-assertive person may require a depth of attitude and behavior development which is possible only in a relationship with a trained therapist.

Juanita, for example, was an "ideal wife"—by some people's standards. She was "maid and mistress" to her husband, doing his every bidding, responding to his slightest whim. A beautiful young woman, Juanita was nevertheless convinced of her own worthlessness. She somehow found herself valuable only as a servant to her husband and infant son. She feared social situations and loneliness and was particularly anxious in enclosed rooms. Her extreme inhibition called for therapeutic intervention on several levels, eventually leading to assertion training. Juanita's husband was at first bewildered, then upset, and finally pleased with her transition from compliant, inhibited servant girl to an independent, self-expressive person. Thus, although a comprehensive set of assertive training situations is included in this book's program for assertiveness development, we are not here attempting to deal with the therapeutic conditions necessary to help the *generally* non-assertive person like Juanita. For such individuals, identified as "generally non-assertive," the best course is to visit a qualified counselor or therapist. Please seek out such help if you need it!

The situational non-asserter may readily recognize his problem and, without too much preparation or prompting, successfully initiate assertion. She/he also has a tendency to recognize ways in life to be assertive with others spontaneously without being specifically instructed to do so. An example is Carol, a 27-year-old college student who told us how others took advantage of her a good deal of the time. Her current difficulty was with a classmate who had borrowed her notes and now had kept them for over a month. The girl needed them back in order to prepare for student teaching and once had even asserted herself to some extent by asking for their return, but the other girl did not return them. The concepts of assertiveness were explained to Carol, the difficulty she had asserting herself properly was pointed out to her, and she role-played calling the girl again, this time being firm and insistent. Within the next few days, she did call the girl, spoke firmly about needing her notes, and soon got them back. In addition, she spoke up to one of her roommates about some matter that upset her. She even complained about an unjust parking ticket and won! In the past, this woman would have let these things slide or pass; however, she learned her lesson quickly. She has continued to assert herself, with a much improved feeling about herself as a result.

In the case of *situational* non-assertiveness, we may assume we are dealing with a relatively healthy person who wishes to develop new ways of handling situations which are now uncomfortable, self-denying, and non-adaptive. If she/he did nothing about these situations, she/he would still be able to function in a relatively healthy manner, but by assertiveness in certain key situations, she/he will make life run more smoothly and feel much more fulfilled as a person. The teacher, counselor, or friend may observe this person's inability to act in his/her own best interest. Or the individual may seek help in overcoming anxiety in a given situation. If you see yourself here, get the help you need. If this book doesn't give you what you want, after diligent practice on your own, please seek professional support.

General and Situational Aggressiveness

"I am the inferior of any man whose rights I trample underfoot," Horace Greeley once stated. In the preceding section, we described the behavior of the person whose anxiety inhibited appropriately assertive responses. Another person may respond to such anxiety by becoming aggressive, "putting himself up" by "putting others down."

It is not uncommon for assertive behavior to be confused with aggressive behavior. We have observed, however, that assertion does not involve hurting another person. Often the aggressive individual *wishes* to stand up for him/herself without hurting others but has not learned appropriate assertive responses. It is easy to misunderstand aggressive acts and to hold low esteem for aggressive people. Although some recent popular books have attempted to improve our understanding of aggressiveness, much remains to be done with this topic. Unfortunately, many popularized, oversimplified and inaccurate explanations, such as those which characterize aggressiveness as "instinctive" in humans, are misleading and of little value in understanding this mode of behavior. It is essential to begin with an acknowledgment of aggression as an inadequate response to anxiety. Hopefully, a recognition of the ease with which one may learn more adaptive assertive responses will reduce out-of-proportion concerns with individual aggression. We will discuss the topic in greater depth in Chapter 10.

The concepts of "general" and "situational" may be applied to aggressive behavior in a fashion similar to our discussion of non-assertiveness. The *generally aggressive* individual is characterized by behavior toward others which is *typically* aggressive in every type of situation. This person appears on the surface to have a high level of self-confidence, to be in command of every situation, to be strong and able to cope with life on his/her own terms. The aggressive male may live according to his image of the American cultural ideal: the aggressive, masculine figure who dominates his environment and demonstrates his "manhood" by bravado. Female aggressiveness is often intellectually oriented: she may typically dominate conversations, belittle the opinions of others, and leave no doubt that she considers herself the final word on nearly any topic.

One who is generally aggressive appears to have friction with the majority of people with whom she/he comes into contact. She/he is extremely sensitive to criticism and feels rejected a good portion of the time. General aggressiveness is characterized by the ease with which one is triggered into aggressive outbursts: in extreme cases, so volatile that the slightest threat to security causes an adverse reaction. The male is often very autocratic in his family relationships, with a submissive wife and cowering children, none of whom dare cross him in any way. He may resort to physical punishment with the children and may be physically abusive with his wife. The generally aggressive person of either sex is often a loner, sullen and moody, who may have great difficulty holding a job.

Because this behavior is so offensive to others, the aggressive person may have few friends and little esteem from his acquaintances. With a need for affection and acceptance as great as anyone's, she/he does not know how to act assertively (and thus gain acceptance) or how to ask for affection. Because of the abusive behavior, attempts at reaching out to others for human contact usually end in frustration and further isolation.

Frank was a generally aggressive person who finally sought help at 39 because his third wife had just threatened to leave him. He had grown up in a "tough" neighborhood, and learned early that aggressive behavior paid off among his peers. He was frequently afraid in encounters with other toughs in the community; however, he never let his fear show, hiding it behind a "bravado" style. As a young adult, he found that some women admired his tough exterior and seemed to enjoy the rough way he treated them. He developed no really close friendships, and married first at 19. After his 17-year-old wife got to know him in the early weeks of the marriage, she ran home, and her parents had the marriage annulled. Frank was hurt, but remained "strong" on the outside. He began to drink heavily and grew increasingly afraid of close relationships. He married again at 24, and managed to keep that union going through six stormy years and the birth of two children. It was his abusive behavior toward the oldest child which led his second wife to divorce him.

Bouncing from job to job over the next several years, at 36 Frank found a widow who broke through his defenses and was genuinely supportive and caring. Her patience with his aggressiveness led him to risk admitting to her some of his fears, and the relationship became quite solid. It was Frank's drunken outburst after a party which resulted in her decision to leave unless he sought professional help. Frank's therapy was intensive and complex, with assertion training—the process of learning constructive self-expression—as only one of several phases. His early learning, resulting in the erroneous idea that being "tough" was the only way to deal with his fears, required a great deal of time and energy to overcome.

Again, as in the case of the generally non-assertive person, we believe the generally aggressive individual is, like Frank, anxious in nearly all social situations. His/her unwillingness or inability to respond to an emotional event honestly, deceiving others and often oneself, calls for a professional therapeutic relationship.

The *situationally aggressive* person responds with aggression only under certain conditions. She/he will usually recognize this condition and may voluntarily seek assistance for the specific problem, or respond readily to another's suggestion of the need to change. This individual may respond positively to the idea of learning a more adaptive response than aggression. Three examples of situational aggressiveness will help place this kind of behavior in clearer perspective.

Jim, a college sophomore, was referred for therapy, being described as having a "chip on his shoulder;" Adele, a senior, was sent for "being too pushy" with an instructor and with her classmates. The young man was a disruptive influence in the classroom: he would ask questions in an aggressive manner which intimidated the teacher, and in class discussions would barge in with his opinions, showing no respect for the opinions of others. Jim's opinionated attitude was offensive, but it was made worse by his contempt for others who did not accept his "obvious" conclusions. He literally disrupted the entire classroom climate by rejecting the validity of any viewpoint other than his own. To say the least, Jim alienated everyone in this classroom situation even though many of his points were well thought out and logical.

Adele only became aggressive after an extended period of non-assertiveness, a very common pattern. As she felt others taking advantage of her more and more, she finally could stand it no longer and would have an aggressive outburst. After such a display of anger, Adele would appear to function well until the build-up occurred again, producing another outburst. Each of these individuals was correct, but ruined the effectiveness of their ideas by inappropriate actions. Both found their academic lives improved by learning how to handle situations assertively.

Another example of situational aggressiveness is that of Pat, 37, who was being counseled with her husband after having worked individually with a therapist for some time. Pat was extremely angry with her husband for his preoccupation with activities outside the home, but she avoided direct confrontation. Instead, her responses to him were "super-sweet," including a direct statement that she "didn't mind" his involvements elsewhere. Nevertheless, Pat did express her bitter resentment by such actions as taking the car when she knew he needed it, cutting him down verbally in front of others, and leaving the children with him when he was particularly busy at home. Such subtly aggressive acts were all a substitute for the honest confrontation Pat would not assert herself to achieve.

"... Sometimes"

Aggressive and non-assertive behavior, then, take many forms. All of us behave aggressively at times, as we do non-assertively as well. To that extent, perhaps we are all *situationally* aggressive or non-assertive, at least on occasion. Still, you should be aware of any *patterns*. Are you regularly avoiding certain people or events because you fear them? Do you often find yourself dominating particular situations? Most important, do these undesired patterns seem to be out of your conscious control?

If behavior you don't want is "happening" too often in your life, if you are not choosing for yourself how you will act, if you don't feel that you are in charge of yourself, and if your inhibition or dominance is not so great as to require professional help (please check that out!), then read on! You are about to find the help you are looking for!

6

"Why Should I Change?"

"Okay," you say, "maybe I am not as assertive as I'd like to be. You can't teach an old dog new tricks. That's just the way I am. I can't change it."

We don't agree. Thousands of persons have found that becoming more assertive is a *learning* process, and that it *was* possible for them to change. Sometimes it takes longer for an "old dog." But the rewards are great, and the process not really that difficult. How do I know that I really want to change in the first place? Are there potential dangers involved in assertion? What about the other people in my life; won't they object if I suddenly become more expressive? This chapter is concerned with laying the ground work for the self-directed development of assertive behavior.

"Yes, I'm non-assertive; so what?" Well, consider, for example, how clearly do you recognize consequences of such behavior? Have you observed how you come across to others? Do people often take advantage of you? Do you avoid certain social situations because you feel too anxious? Have you lost out on a job because you couldn't bring yourself to talk to someone? Has it ever cost you money because you "just couldn't" take a faulty item back to a store? Do you own some things you don't want because you "couldn't say no"? Have you been criticized by your spouse or others for indecisiveness?

Any of these consequences of non-assertiveness is bound to produce personal anguish, disappointment, perhaps self-recrimination. If you have experienced this kind of pain, you already have felt the motivation to change. You are ready to get on with it, and we are convinced that the procedure presented here will be of great value to you. Learning to express "your perfect right" is not a cure-all, but it is a big step toward freeing yourself from the burdens of self-denying behavior.

It is often more difficult for the aggressive person to acknowledge a need for help, since she/he is accustomed to controlling the environment to suit his/her own needs. If aggressiveness is your style, you may wish to consider that your present relationships may become worse unless you seek change. Unhealthy relationships tend to deteriorate and may leave you feeling worse than you do now. Generally, we have found that the aggressive person who seeks to change does so as a result of the suggestion of others—or is moved by frustration with the inadequacy of his/her responses.

Do you always take the lead in social relationships? Do you find that you continually have to call first in making contact with friends? Do others seldom engage you in discussion willingly? Are you invariably the "winner" in arguments? Do you often berate clerks and waitresses for inadequate service? Are you the "ruler" of your subordinates on the job? Of your family at home? Do you find people trying to "get back" at you? Alienation of those close to you is a high price to pay for having things go your own way. Assertiveness can often achieve the same ends, with fewer casualties in your relationships.

One example which interestingly demonstrates both non-assertive and aggressive responses to anxiety is the case of young Caren, who was having fits of anger which were expressed toward the man she planned to marry. Her anxiety was caused by his lack of consideration; he would be late for dates, not inform her until the last minute about engagements he wanted her to attend with him, and show other similar discourtesies. Caren would not assert her right to demand due courtesy until her anger had built up to an irritational level: then she would explode at him. Once she was aware that the situation would likely only grow worse after marriage, and could imagine the possibility of her marriage ending in divorce, Caren agreed to assertive training. Unfortunately, many women go through their entire marriage "under the thumb" of their husbands because they feel it is "their place" in the marriage relationship.

Stand Up for Your Perfect Rights

When suggesting assertion to individuals, we emphasize the fact that no one has a right to take advantage of another simply on a human-being-to-human-being level. For instance, an employer has no right to take advantage of an employee's natural rights to courtesy and respect as a human being. A doctor does not have the right to be discourteous or unfair in dealing with a patient or nurse. A lawyer should not patronizingly "talk down" to a laborer. Each person has a perfect right to speak his piece even though she/he may "only have a grade (or high) school education" or be "from the wrong side of the tracks" or be "just a secretary." All persons are indeed created equal on a human-to-human plane; and each deserves the privilege of expressing those "inalienable" rights. There is so much more to be gained from life by being free and able to stand up for oneself, and from honoring the same right for others. By being assertive, one is actually learning to give and take more equally with others and to be of more service to self and others.

Another reason which motivates many to become assertive is the likelihood that somatic ailments will be reduced as assertion progresses. Complaints such as headaches, asthma, gastric disorders, and general fatigue often clear up. The reduction in guilt and anxiety which is experienced by non-assertive and aggressive persons who learn to be assertive often results in the elimination of such physical symptoms.

This is a good time to realize that you are not alone —that others have faced similar challenges and situations and have changed for the better!

The hope and courage necessary for a non-assertive person to initiate training may be bolstered by studying case descriptions to learn how others successfully overcame similar difficulties. Read Andrew Salter's comments in his book, *Conditioned Reflex Therapy,* to find examples of your own inhibitions. Ask yourself how readily you could accept the advice given in each situation.

The aggressive person, on the other hand, is encouraged to read Bach and Wyden's *The Intimate Enemy* (particularly Chapters 6, 9, and 13). You may be able to "see yourself" in one of these descriptions of others, and as a result desire to overcome this problem. You probably "see yourself" in examples we have already given or will provide later in this book.

One implication of assertion recurs time and again with non-assertive individuals: self-denying behavior subtly reinforces the other person's bad or unwanted behavior. Two examples help to make this point clear:

Diane, a married woman of 35, had a husband who desired sexual intercourse every evening. At times she would clearly be tired from the day's activities as a housewife and mother of three and not wish intercourse. However, when Diane would refuse him, her husband would begin to pout and feel hurt, carrying on until she would finally "feel sorry" for him and give in. This sequence was a consistent pattern in their marriage. The more Diane would not give in, the more he would pout until she did so. Of course, by eventually giving in she promptly reinforced all of his pouting, not to mention the reinforcement value of his sexual gratification!

Another example concerns a college student. Wendy, age 20, although surviving quite well on her own, was a self-styled "hippie," living off-campus in a cheap habitat with another girl and a boy. By living together they cut expenses and saved a good deal of money. Wendy and her roommates had a reputation for being "anti-administration." Word of her behavior and style of living got back to her parents, who then confronted her with a long tirade about the younger generation, respect for authority, her mother's health, her lack of respect, and so on. This happened on several occasions, and each time Wendy would eventually get upset and either ask what she could do to help ease things or simply give in to some of their demands. Here again, by her response of getting upset and giving in, Wendy simply reinforced her parents' unwanted behavior; that is, *she taught them* how to have these tirades against her.

Although it may be more difficult for the aggressive individual to admit the negative consequences of his/her actions, one usually recognizes the reactions others have to denial of their rights. She/he reacts internally with acknowledgment and pain when confronted with the alienation this behavior brings about. If you are seeking help, you may admit to yourself your concern and guilt over the hurt you cause others and acknowledge that you simply do not know how to gain your goals non-aggressively. At this point you are an excellent candidate for assertive training.

One individual of this type was "reached" in a therapy group setting. After considerable time had been spent listening to Jerry's loud dominance over the group, several members took him to task. Although he was a large, rugged man, Jerry soon responded to this *caring but confronting* response by the others and began to cry. He confessed that he had developed this façade of bravado to protect himself from the interpersonal closeness which he feared. He really felt himself to be quite an inadequate person, and had used the "strong man" mask to keep others at a distance. The group responded to Jerry's need for others to care for him and later helped him to shape adequately assertive responses to replace his previously gruff, bellicose behavior.

A Game Plan for Your Assertiveness: When and Where

Once you are well motivated and ready to begin asserting yourself, you must *first* make certain that you understand thoroughly the basic principles of assertion. Realizing differences between assertive and aggressive behavior is important to your understanding and success.

Second, you must decide whether you are ready to begin trying self-assertive behavior on your own. Usually *situationally non-assertive* or *situationally aggressive* persons are able to begin assertion quite successfully.

With the *generally non-assertive* and *generally aggressive,* however, more caution is involved and we recommend slow and careful practice and work, either with another person—preferably a trained therapist—as a facilitator, or in a group with a qualified counselor or leader.

Third, your initial attempts at being assertive should be made in situations where you are likely to be successful, so as to provide reinforcement. This point, of course, is important with all beginning asserters, but especially the *generally non-assertive* and *generally aggressive*. The more successfully you assert yourself at first, the more likely you are to be successful from that point on.

Begin with small assertions that are likely to be rewarding, and from there proceed to more difficult assertions. You may wish to explore each step with a friend or trained facilitator until you are capable of being fully in control of most situations. Be careful not to attempt a difficult assertion without special preparation. And be especially careful not to instigate an assertion where you are likely to fail miserably, thus inhibiting your further attempts at assertiveness.

If you do suffer a setback, which may very well happen, take time to analyze the situation carefully and regain your confidence, getting help from a facilitator if necessary. Especially in the early stages of assertion, it is not unusual to make mistakes either of inadequate technique or of overzealousness to the point of aggression. Either miscue could cause negative returns, particularly if the other individual, the person "acted upon," becomes hostile and highly aggressive. Don't let such an occurrence stop you. Keep your goal in mind, and remember that although successful assertiveness requires practice, the rewards are great.

Fourth, give some thought to your relationships with those who are closest to you. Typically, patterns of non-assertive or aggressive behavior have been operational in an individual for a long period of time. The non-asserter will have well-established patterns of interaction with those significantly close to him, such as family, spouse, and friends. So will the aggressive person. A change in these established relationships will very likely be upsetting to the others involved.

Parents are often targets of assertive behavior, especially during the late teens and early twenties, when children are striving for independence. Of course, some people defer to their parents' wishes and commands as long as they are living (because it is the "right thing" to do to respect one's elders, primarily parents, who sacrificed so much for you, etc.). Many parents believe this line of thinking and therefore are likely to be quite disconcerted when their child "rebels" assertively. On the other hand, parents who have patterned their lives in response to an aggressive child could be equally unsettled to find his behavior changing to assertive, even though they have often wished for such a day. Consequently, it may be valuable to ask a facilitator to intervene and talk to the parents to prepare them for what is to come. This intervention can often prevent their reactions from becoming exacerbated, and can avoid causing deeply strained relations between parents and child.

Marriage relationships which have been based for years upon the non-assertive or aggressive actions of one partner are similarly apt to be upset when assertion commences. If the spouse is not properly prepared and willing to change to some degree himself, a marital break-up is a definite possibility. Cooperation from the spouse through one or more conferences with a facilitator can help a great deal to cushion the change in behavior. Hopefully, assertive training for one spouse will also strengthen the marital relationship.

A woman who complained for years of her husband's lack of firmness in dealing with others became upset when he finally sought help, participated in assertiveness training, and began to stand up to *her*. She could not accept his new behavior and told him she didn't know if she loved him any more. Fortunately, the couple saw the therapist together and were able to work out a new "balance" in their marriage. There is naturally a potential for damage to an intimate relationship from significant behavior change by one partner, and caution must be observed in proceeding with these likely consequences in mind.

"Okay ... I'm Ready"

If you have carefully reviewed the cautions noted in this chapter and consider yourself ready to develop new assertiveness, the next two chapters present the process that we and our colleagues have found effective with thousands of persons who have sought to become more assertive. The process is at once very simple and very difficult. Take it slowly, step by step, building on your own successes. You'll find it works for you, too.

If, however, you find the cautions we have suggested seem to present too formidable a barrier, we suggest you seek out a therapist who is willing to help you with your growth. Find someone whom you can trust, perhaps someone you already know or who is recommended by a friend, physician, or minister. Discuss your concerns about becoming more assertive. Try to understand the price you pay for remaining non-assertive or aggressive. If you genuinely *choose* to continue in that style of behavior, even though you are aware of the costs to you and to your relationships with others, by all means do so. On the other hand, if, as we suspect, you find that fear of change is holding you back, please use your therapist to aid you in overcoming that fear. The long-term rewards are well worth the effort!

Ready now? If you've come this far, you are probably prepared to begin taking steps toward increasing your own assertiveness. We know you can succeed. The rewards far exceed the effort required.

II

The Assertiveness Training Program

. . . There are three possible broad approaches to the conduct of interpersonal relations. The first is to consider one's self only and ride roughshod over others. . . . The second . . . is always to put others before one's self. . . . The third approach is the golden mean. . . . The individual places himself first, but takes others into account.

—Joseph Wolpe, M.D.,
The Practice of Behavior Therapy

7

Your Journey to Assertiveness

Perhaps you have heard it said that "when two engineers [lawyers, housewives, plumbers, nurses] are talking together and a psychologist walks up and joins the conversation, there are now two engineers and a psychologist; but when two psychologists are talking and an engineer [substitute your own favorite] walks up and joins them, there are now three psychologists!" Everyone believes he is a psychologist in some sense. Indeed, we all have some practical, first-hand knowledge of human behavior, beginning with ourselves.

Changing Your Behavior and Attitudes

Unfortunately, there are occasional shortcomings in generally held views of how people behave. One popular view which has been found by psychologists to be inaccurate is the notion that one must change his attitude before he can change the way he acts. In our experience with hundreds of clients in clinical assertive training, and in the feedback from some of the thousands of readers of this book, as well as from countless reports from our colleagues in psychological practice and research, it is now clear that *behavior can be changed first,* and it is easier and more effective to do so in most cases.

As you begin the process of becoming more assertive,

we won't ask you to wake up some morning and say, "Today I am a new, assertive person!" You will find here instead a guide to systematic, step-by-step changes in behavior. The key to developing assertiveness is *practice of new behavior patterns*. This chapter is devoted to leading you through the steps involved in such practice, and showing how you can put the newly assertive behavior to work in your relationships with others.

We have observed a cycle of non-assertive or aggressive behavior which tends to perpetuate itself, until a decisive intervention occurs. A person who has acted non-assertively or aggressively in his relationships for a long period of time usually thinks poorly of himself. His behavior toward others—whether self-denying or abusive—evokes scorn, disdain, avoidance. He observes the response and says to himself, "See, I knew I was no damn good." Confirmed in his low self-evaluation, he continues his inadequate behavior patterns. Thus the cycle is repeated: inadequate behavior; negative feedback; attitude of self-depreciation; inadequate behavior.

The most readily observable component of this pattern is the *behavior* itself. We can easily see overt behavior in contrast with attitudes and feelings which may be hidden behind a practiced façade. In addition, *behavior* is the component most amenable to change. Our efforts to facilitate improved interpersonal functioning and a greater valuing of yourself as a person will focus on changing your *behavior* patterns.

We find the cycle can be reversed, becoming a positive sequence: more adequately assertive (self-enhancing) behavior gains more positive responses from others; this positive feedback leads to an enhanced evaluation of self-worth ("Wow, people are treating me like a worthwhile person!"); and improved feelings about oneself result in further assertiveness.

Harold had for years been convinced that he was truly

worthless. He was totally dependent upon his wife for emotional support, and despite a rather handsome appearance and an ability to express himself well, he had literally no friends. Imagine his utter despair when his wife left him! Fortunately, Harold was already in therapy at the time and was willing to try to make contact with other people. When his first attempts at assertiveness with eligible young women were successful beyond his wildest hopes, the reinforcing value of such responses to his assertions was very high. Harold's entire outlook toward himself changed rapidly, and he became much more assertive in a variety of situations.

Not everyone, to be sure, will experience such an immediate "payoff" for his/her assertions, and not all assertions are fully successful. Success often requires a great deal of patience, and a gradual process of handling more and more difficult situations. Nevertheless this example emphasizes a general rule we have found in facilitating assertive behavior: *assertiveness tends to be self-rewarding*. It feels good when others begin to respond to you more attentively, when you achieve your goals in relationships, when you find situations going your way more often. *And you can make these changes happen!*

Remember to begin with assertions where you have a good chance of success before proceeding to more difficult ones requiring greater confidence and skill. It is often helpful and reassuring to obtain support and guidance from another person, perhaps a friend, teacher, or professional therapist.

Mary, a member of one of our assertive behavior groups, just yesterday (as this is written) commented upon how much her *attitude* toward relating to others has changed as a result of taking part in the group. She now feels supported in acting assertively, in expressing herself and standing up for her rights. For Mary, that *authorization* of assertive behavior is more important even than the *practice* which the group also provides. Although we know that the process of learning a new style for relating to others, the practice of new behaviors, is the key to *starting someone out* toward new assertiveness, we have often heard comments like Mary's from persons who are becoming more effectively assertive.

It is as if throughout one's life, people in authority (parents, teachers, other adults, even powerful peers) have been saying "You have no right. . . ." Now, someone in apparent "authority"—a psychologist, a university faculty member, a doctor—is saying "You have a *perfect right.* . . ." That legitimizing of self-expression is a powerful part of our message to you. It's *good,* it's *right,* it's *okay* to assert yourself!

Keep in mind that changed behavior leads to changed attitudes about one's self and one's impact upon people and situations. The balance of this chapter presents the steps involved in bringing about that changed behavior. Read *all* the material here carefully *before* you begin. Then return to this point and begin to follow the steps in your own life. You'll like the difference in you!

The Step-by-Step Process

Step 1: Observe your own behavior. Are you asserting yourself adequately? Are you satisfied with your effectiveness in interpersonal relationships? Look over the discussion in Chapter 2 again, and assess how *you* feel about yourself and your behavior.

Step 2: Keep track of your assertiveness. Make a log or diary for a week. Record each day those situations in which you found yourself responding assertively, those in which you "blew it," and those you avoided altogether so that you would not have to face the need to act assertively. Be honest with yourself, and systematic!

Step 3: Concentrate on a particular situation. Spend a few moments with your eyes closed, imagining how you handle a specific incident (being shortchanged at the supermarket, having a friend "talk your ear off" on the telephone when you had too much to do, letting the boss make you "feel like 2¢" over a small mistake). Imagine vividly the actual details, including your specific feelings at the time and afterward.

Step 4: Review your responses. Write down your behavior in Step 3 in terms of the components of assertiveness noted in Chapter 8 (eye contact, body posture, gestures, facial expression, voice, timing, fluency, message content). Look carefully at the components of your behavior in the recalled incident. Note your strengths. Be aware of those components which represent non-assertive or aggressive behavior.

Step 5: Observe an effective model. At this point it would be very helpful to watch someone who handles the same situation very well. Watch for the components discussed in Chapter 8, particularly the *style*—the words are less important. If the model is a friend, discuss his/her approach, and its consequences.

Step 6: Consider alternative responses. What are other possible ways the incident could be handled? Could you deal with it more to your own advantage? Less offensively? Refer to the chart in Chapter 4, and differentiate between non-assertive, aggressive, and assertive responses.

Step 7: Imagine yourself handling the situation. Close your eyes and visualize yourself dealing effectively with the situation. You may act similarly to the "model" in Step 5, or in a very different way. Be assertive, but be as much your "natural self" as you can. Repeat this step as often as necessary until you can imagine a comfortable style for yourself which succeeds in handling the situation well.

Step 8: Try it out. Having examined your own behavior, considered alternatives, and observed a model of more adaptive action, you are now prepared to begin trying out for yourself new ways of dealing with the problem situation. A repeat of Steps 5, 6, and 7 may be appropriate until you are ready to proceed. It is important to select an alternative, more effective way of behaving in problem situations. You may wish to follow your model and enact the same approach taken by him or her in Step 5. Such a choice is appropriate, but remember that you are a unique person, and the model's approach may not be one which you feel good about adopting for yourself. In that case, select a more effective alternative behavior and try it out in a role-playing situation with a friend, teacher, or therapist, attempting to act in accord with the new response pattern you have selected. As in Steps 2, 3, and 4, make careful observation of your behavior, using available mechanical recording aids whenever possible.

Step 9: Get feedback. This step essentially repeats Step 4 with emphasis on the positive aspects of your behavior. Note particularly the strengths of your performance, and work positively to improve weaker areas.

Step 10: Behavior shaping. Steps 7, 8, and 9 should be repeated as often as necessary to "shape" your behavior—by this process of successive approximations of your goal—to a point wherein you feel comfortable dealing in a self-enhancing manner with the previously threatening situation.

Step 11: The real test. You are now ready to test your new response pattern in the actual situation. Up to this point your preparation has taken place in a relatively secure environment. Nevertheless, careful training and repeated practice have prepared you to react almost automatically to the situation. You should thus be encouraged to proceed with a real-life trial. If you are unwilling to do so, further rehearsals may be needed. (Persons who are chronically anxious and insecure, or who seriously doubt their own self-worth, may need professional therapy. You are strongly urged to seek professional assistance if you believe it is indicated.) Again, remember that *doing*, honestly, spontaneously, is the most important step of all.

Step 12: Further training. You are encouraged to repeat the procedures that you find helpful in the development of the behavior you desire. You may also wish to start a similar practice program for dealing with other specific situations in which you wish to develop an assertive response. Chapters 4, 12, 13, 14, 15, and 16 describe some examples which may be helpful in planning your own program for change.

Step 13: Social reinforcement. As a final step in establishing an independent behavior pattern, it is very important that you understand the need for continual self-reinforcement. In order to maintain your newly developed assertive behavior, you should seek out reinforcements in your own social environment. For example, you now know the good feeling which accom-

panies a successful assertion and you can rest assured
that this good response will continue. Admiration received from others will be another continuing positive
response to your growth. You may wish to develop a
checklist of reinforcements which are unique to your
own environment. Chapter 17 has some ideas which
may help you to make up your list.

In conclusion, although we emphasize the importance
of this systematic learning process, it should be understood that what is recommended is not a lock-step,
forced pattern without consideration for the needs and
objectives of each individual. You are encouraged to
provide a learning environment which will help you to
grow in assertiveness. No one system is "right" for
everyone. We encourage you to be systematic, but to
follow a program which will meet your own unique individual needs. There is, of course, no substitute for the
active practice of assertive behavior in your own life,
when *you* choose to, as a means of developing greater
assertiveness and enjoying its accompanying rewards.

"But What If It Doesn't Work?"

There are going to be failures in your attempts at assertion. We surely do not claim that these procedures will
turn you into an instant 100 per cent success in all your
relationships with others. As we have said, there are no
magic answers to all of life's problems. We, too, find
that assertiveness does not always work!

Occasionally, for example, your goals will simply be
mutually incompatible with the other person's. If you are
both headed for the same parking space, someone has
to give! At times, the other person may be unreasonable
or unyielding, and your best assertions (or *ours!*) would
not move him/her.

Moreover, you too are human. You'll blow it some-times. We all do. Allow yourself to make mistakes! Sure, it's uncomfortable, you wish you had done it dif-ferently, you're disappointed, down, discouraged. Allow yourself that humanness, then pick yourself up and try again. You'll find, as did strike-out *and* home-run king Babe Ruth, that if you are going to hit the ball, you've got to keep swinging the bat!

If you find your assertions are failing a bit too often, take stock of what's going on. Are you setting your sights too high? Make your goals *achievable* and take small steps to insure success! Are you overdoing it and becoming aggressive? Monitor your behavior carefully —keep referring to Chapter 8 and check yourself. (In-cidentally, some aggression at first is to be expected from the formerly non-assertive. You'll find a balance in a short time.)

Finally, although you want your assertions to work, and you want to achieve your goals, remember that the greatest value of self-assertion is the good feeling of having expressed yourself. To know, as our group mem-ber Mary does now, that you are a person of value who has a *perfect right* to self-expression, and to feel free to go ahead and say what you're feeling, and to *do* it are the most important benefits of all.

Usually you'll find your new assertiveness *will* make these things happen. But if not, remember how good it felt to speak up for yourself! You know you have done what you could, even if the outcome isn't what you hoped for. Keep in mind how little chance there is to achieve your desired outcomes when you do *nothing!*

Do It!

Now that you know what is involved in the process of developing assertive behavior, don't allow yourself to remain a passive observer. If you are interested enough to have read this far, you are either thinking seriously about improving your own assertiveness or considering how you can help others to become more assertive. In either case, *do something about it!* You cannot change solely by sitting there reading this book. If we don't move you to action in your own life, we have served only as a diversion and we are disappointed. If, on the other hand, you go out now and handle *one* interpersonal situation more in your own best interests, we are pleased to have had a part in your growth.

Try it! (You'll like it!)

8 _____

"But I Never Know What To Say!"

It almost doesn't matter *what* you say! Of the several components of an assertive message, we have discovered that *what* you say is a good deal less important than *how* you say it. Consider this example: You purchased a sweater ten days ago in a relatively expensive clothing store. After wearing it only twice, you notice that a sleeve has begun to unravel. Picture yourself returning the sweater to the store and saying, "I bought this sweater here ten days ago, and now it's unravelling. I'd like a new sweater or my money back."

How did you present yourself? *Using the same words* in each case, consider the relative impact of your message if:

(1) You walk up to the counter hesitatingly, look down at the floor frequently while speaking, talk almost in a whisper, maintain a fearful expression, put your hands in your pockets or grip the package tightly, and stoop over slightly while turned sideways to the clerk;

(2) You stride up to the counter, glare at the clerk, speak in loud tones and shake your fist, face the clerk squarely and draw up to your full height;

(3) You walk briskly up to the counter, smile pleasantly while looking directly at the clerk, speak in a conversational tone, maintain a calm, firm expression, gesture to point out the flaw or add emphasis, and face

the clerk squarely while standing naturally and comfortably.

The difference in the three approaches is obvious. The first, representative of our "non-assertive" style, is a self-demeaning posture, sure to reveal you to the clerk as a pushover, destined to be denied your rightful due because you appear to be an "easy mark." In the second (aggressive) case, you probably will get what you're after (the refund), but almost certainly the clerk will detest you and make the process as prolonged and unpleasant as possible. Approach (3) will in all likelihood achieve your goal, and the clerk (and whomever you may be with) will respect you for it.

The message here is that in many instances the non-verbal aspects of your behavior say more than do the words themselves. Although we don't really believe the words are *unimportant,* they are most certainly less important than many people believe. The fact that you assert yourself is primary, the way you handle it is next, and finally, what you say is of less importance.

In the past decade considerable research has been done in the area of non-verbal dimensions of communication. We now have evidence to demonstrate the manner in which we utilize these components of behavior to establish territoriality, dominance, relationship, emphasis, interest, caring, control, approval, recognition.

Watch some people expressing themselves. One effective way to do this is to watch a dramatic production on television with the sound turned down so you can't hear what is being said. Almost invariably you can detect the mood and some of the message of the speakers by noting their eye contact, facial expression, gestures, posture, etc.

Let's consider each of these components in greater detail.

Eye Contact

Looking directly at another person to whom you are speaking is an effective way of declaring that you are sincere about what you are saying, and that it is directed to that person. Looking away or looking down suggests a lack of confidence in oneself or deference to the other person. An aggressive stare may be an attempt to "overpower" the other. Continuous eye contact can be uncomfortable, inappropriate, or even a "game;" but a relaxed, steady gaze into the other's eyes, punctuated by occasional looking away, personalizes communication and emphasizes your interest in that person.

The conscious use of eye contact is relatively simple to develop. Pay attention to your eye communication as you converse with others. Try to increase your eye attention. Don't overdo it, but let the other person know you are interested by looking at him/her, not at the floor, walls, or out the window as you are talking and listening.

Body Posture

The "weight" of your messages to others will be increased if you face the person, stand or sit appropriately close, lean toward him/her, and hold your head erect. We are continually amazed to observe the number of persons who maintain conversations—usually briefly!—while their entire bodies are aimed away from each other! For example, as two people sit beside each other, on an airplane, on a couch, in a classroom, at dinner, it is almost typical that each will face straight ahead for nearly all of the time, turning only the head slightly toward the other. A simple turn of the shoulders, say 30°, toward the other makes the conversation so much more personal! Interest in the other person is clearly demonstrated by this simple change of posture.

In a "stand up for yourself" assertive encounter, leaning toward the other presents a stronger case than leaning away. Also, an active, erect posture lends assertion to your communication, in contrast to a passive, slumping stance. Observing your own posture and your distance from others in conversation will help you to identify the effect of your own "physical presence."

Gestures

A message accented with appropriate gestures takes on added emphasis. Dr. Alberti is fond of referring to the importance of gestures in his Italian heritage. Latins typically utilize extensive gesturing to *describe* a scene or object visually as well as verbally, and to *emphasize* specific points in communication. While over-enthusiastic gesturing can be a distraction, a relaxed use of hands and arms while talking adds depth to the message and avoids the awkward stiffness of arms folded or straight at your sides. Particularly powerful gestures include the angry fist shaken at your adversary, a soft hand on the arm or shoulder, an open hand extended in front of you ("Stop!").

Another important aspect of gesturing is its message that the speaker is relatively uninhibited, and therefore apparently self-confident. Freedom of arm and hand movements usually accompanies a willingness to express oneself freely, a lack of inhibition, a sense of personal power. Certain nervous gestures, of course, can have precisely the opposite effect, so it is important to develop expressive purposeful gestures which are congruent with your feelings and your verbal message. Such physical expression can be very helpful in increasing the spontaneity of your communication as well.

Facial Expression

Have you ever seen someone trying to express anger while smiling or laughing? Often persons who are very nervous about expressing anger will show their anxiety in a smile. Result: the anger just doesn't come across! Effective assertions require an expression that agrees with the message.

Right now, try looking at yourself in the mirror. Now smile as broadly as you can Hold the pose. Pay attention to the feeling of tightness in your face as you exercise the smile muscles. Notice your expression in the mirror. Study the lines in your cheeks and around your eyes. Now relax your face Release the tightness in the smile muscles. Let go of the tightness, and let your jaw relax. Keep on letting go until your jaw goes slack and your mouth opens slightly. Pay attention to the difference in the feeling in your face and the difference in your expression in the mirror.

As you become more aware of the feelings in your face, you can better control your expression. When you want to appear firm, and/or angry, you won't smile, but will adopt a stern expression consistent with your feelings. Your smile can become more natural, and less the automatic, plastic face it may have been.

Voice Tone, Inflection, Volume

A whispered monotone will seldom convince another person that you mean business, while a shouted epithet will bring his defenses into the path of communication. A level, well-modulated conversational statement is convincing without intimidating.

It is relatively simple to get direct feedback about how your voice sounds to others. Most people have access to some sort of tape recorder, and you can try out your voice in several different styles. A regular conversational tone—perhaps reading some prose—will give you a "base line." Then try an angry blast at a make-believe enemy. Then a supportive, caring message. Try persuading someone to accept your point of view.

Each of these samples of your own voice will help you to see how you use your voice to express your feelings. Voice is one of our most valuable resources for communication. When you listen to yourself, pay attention to the *tone* of your voice. Does it have a raspy sharpness when you're angry? Does that change to a soft smoothness to express caring? How about the conversational quality?

Second, notice the inflection. Do you speak in a monotone? Or perhaps with a "sing-song" modulation? Does your inflection really emphasize what you want it to? Finally, how about volume? Do you ordinarily speak so softly that others can barely hear? That can be a subtle means of controlling people, by forcing them to listen carefully. Can you bring out a shout when you *want* to? Or is your conversational volume so loud that people think you're *always* angry?

Get control of your voice, and you'll have harnessed a powerful element of your developing assertiveness!

Fluency

Hesitation in speech is a signal to others that you are unsure of yourself. You need not be a polished speaker in order to get your point across, but you are encouraged to work at making your speech flow smoothly. Comments spoken clearly and slowly are more powerful than rapid, erratic speech filled with stammering and hesitation.

You can practice fluency with a tape recorder. First think of a subject about which you have some knowledge. Then speak into the recorder's microphone on that subject for thirty seconds. Your own words, please —no reading here! Now listen to the recording. Notice particularly the pauses—3 seconds or more of silence— and the "space fillers"—"uhh . . ." and "you know." Now try the same commentary again—speak more slowly if necessary—this time try to do the entire thirty seconds with no significant pauses, and without resorting to fillers. Keep on practicing this until you can easily handle the thirty seconds on a topic you know well. Then begin on a more difficult topic. Then on to an assertion, and so on until you are satisfied that your fluency is a genuine asset in your efforts at self-expression.

Timing

Spontaneous expression will generally be your goal, since hesitation may diminish the effect of an assertion. Judgment is necessary, however, to *select* an appropriate occasion—such as speaking to your boss in the privacy of his office, rather than in front of a group of his subordinates where he may need to respond defensively.

Indeed, although spontaneity is generally best, it is also true that to confront someone before a group will usually bring his/her defenses up. No one enjoys "looking bad" or being wrong in front of others. Creating an opportunity to talk with the person alone is advised in such an event. Your assertion is more likely to succeed, and the other person will not harbor ill feelings stemming from embarrassment.

Don't worry about being "too late" to express yourself. Even if your assertion cannot change anything now, go ahead. If you harbor resentment over something past, it will eat away at you, and diminish the relationship. It's never too late. More on this in Chapter 9.

Content

We save this obvious dimension of assertiveness for last to emphasize that, although *what* you say is clearly important, it is often *less* important than most of us generally believe. We encourage a fundamental honesty in interpersonal communication, and spontaneity of expression. In our view, that means saying forcefully, "I'm damn mad about what you just did!" rather than "You're an S.O.B.!" People who have for years hesitated because they "didn't know *what* to say" have found the practice of saying *something,* to express their feelings *at the time,* to be a valuable step toward greater spontaneous assertiveness. A big vocabulary is *not* necessary—say what *you feel!*

One further word about content. We do encourage you to express your own feelings—and to *accept responsibility for them.* Note the difference in the above example between "I'm mad" and "You're an S.O.B." It is not necessary to put the other person down (aggressive) in order to express *your* feeling (assertive).

Your imagination can carry you to a wide variety of situations which demonstrate the importance of the *manner* in which you *express* your assertions. Let it suffice to say here that the time you may be spending *thinking about* "just the right words" will be better spent *making* those assertions! The ultimate goal is expressing *yourself,* honestly and spontaneously, in a manner "right" for you.

9

"It's Too Late Now!"

Clients in assertive therapy or members of our assertiveness training groups often talk about situations which have occurred in the past. Although they are frustrated by the consequences of their earlier lack of assertion, they feel that they can do nothing about the problem "at this late date," and believe they are helpless to change the situation now.

An example of such a case involved the relationship of Henry R, an executive, and his secretary, Charlotte B. Henry found himself regularly completing letters and reports late in the day, and asking Charlotte to have them typed and duplicated for meetings the following morning. The first time she was asked to remain after hours to complete the work, the secretary assumed that the request was due to unique circumstances. She willingly agreed to help out. Later Charlotte found the "special request" had become an expectation, and occurred two or three times a week. Although she enjoyed the work, her personal life was being interfered with, and she began to think about quitting her job. Fortunately, she sought help in an assertiveness training group, where she somewhat tentatively brought the subject up for discussion. She found the therapist and group members supported her feeling of imposition. She selected a relatively assertive man in the group and "rehearsed" with him a scene in which she confronted the boss with her feelings. She did poorly at first, apologizing and allowing the boss to convince her that such "loyalty to the company" was necessary to her job. With feedback and support from the group, however, Charlotte improved her ability to express her feelings effectively and not be cowed by the executive's response. The next day, Charlotte confronted Mr. R at the office, made her point, and arranged with him a more reasonable schedule for such projects. In the two months following, Henry made "special requests" only twice, and only when the circumstances clearly *were* unusual. Both were pleased with the result.

The point here is that it is seldom too late for an appropriate assertion—even if a situation has grown worse over some time. Approaching the person involved—yes, even a family member, spouse, lover, boss, employee—with an honest "I've been concerned about _____ for some time" or "I've been wanting to talk with you about _____" can lead to resolution of an uncomfortable issue. And, as no small side benefit, it can open communication of feelings in the future.

Keep in mind the importance of stating your feelings in such a way as to accept responsibility for them: "I'm concerned . . ." *not* "You've got me upset . . . ;" "I'm mad . . ." *not* "You made me mad. . . ."

We are convinced of the value of keeping your life "clear." Again, you have had experiences in which someone has made you angry, taken unfair advantage, or otherwise hurt you. Perhaps you were unable or unwilling to do or say anything about it. Yet those feelings of resentment don't just go away. They continue to eat at you and to damage further the relationship you have with that person. The gap tends to widen, or the mistrust grows, and the relationship deteriorates until something is done.

Joyce was a married woman of 24 who admitted, in therapy, her resentment toward her father for his extremely strict treatment of her as a teenager. She had felt completely untrusted and had been denied any freedom or responsibility for herself. As a result, she believed, her relationship with her husband Bill had suffered measurably. She continued to act toward Bill as though she had to measure up to her father's arbitrary standards. Bill did not understand her inhibition or her lack of self-esteem. He cared for her a great deal and wanted very much to make Joyce happy.

After Joyce recognized her feelings toward her father, she decided to clear up the relationship by talking with him about it. Although she approached him with much apprehension, she discovered that he too had felt badly about his own behavior in earlier years, but did not want to reopen the old wounds, so he hadn't mentioned it to Joyce. Once the subject was out in the open, both Joyce and her father were much relieved, and Joyce found herself able to begin relating to Bill as an independent adult.

Much of the process of growing up revolves around the resolution of the issue of independence from our parents. Typically, and in the healthiest case, the rebelliousness of teenagers is a normal developmental process which facilitates the growing independence of the youngster. Unfortunately, that breaking away is sometimes prevented, in Joyce's case by her father's dominance over her every act. Some teenagers are themselves too fearful and dependent to take the necessary steps. In either case, adults of all ages may find the parent tie still restricting their lives as independent human beings. We have found that an assertive approach to the parent by the "child" can make the situation clear, and allow both parties to express their feelings.

To open up such old wounds is to take a considerable

risk of emotional pain for both parent and child; nevertheless we consider the price of continued silence to be too high. Untold suffering, guilt, self-denial, inhibition, repressed anger, and attempts to compensate have resulted for millions of people who have avoided dealing with their parents or adult children as they would with any other adult. Once again, it is *not* too late! (Therapists have devised special techniques for helping even those whose parents have died with the conflict unresolved.)

Similarly, in other ongoing relationships, among friends, co-workers or neighbors, feelings of resentment for actions in the past tend to create further ill will and to destroy closeness and good feeling. Hazel and Carolyn, co-workers in an accounting office, got into an argument over correct procedures for posting the accounts. The two had worked together for several years, and the current dispute threatened what had been a very positive working relationship. For over a month since the disagreement came into the open, they had been barely civil to each other. Carolyn, who had been the "underdog" in the office, actually had enjoyed working with Hazel, but felt the disagreement had gone on "too long to do anything about it now," and was depressed about having to work with these "bad vibes" in the office.

With the encouragement of a more assertive friend, Carolyn gained the courage to confront Hazel with her feelings. "I still don't agree about the posting procedure, Hazel," she began, "but I like you, and I really hope we can be friends again. Even friends can disagree!" Hazel was reluctant: "I don't think you see the importance of this, Carolyn." "Yes, I do," Carolyn responded with determination, "but I think our working relationship can survive this difference of opinion. We both have to live with the supervisor's decision anyway.

I'm upset about what has happened—even a little angry with you still—but I want us to try to work it out." Hazel softened: "Well, I suppose I feel the same way. And we do have to work together. Let's talk it over at lunch. . . ."

Perhaps not always so simply or successfully as Hazel and Carolyn, disputes of long standing *can* be resolved or set aside and friendships restored. Angry or hurt feelings *can* and *should* be brought up at a late date, so that the more important priorities—human relationships—can be revived. Going back to resolve an old conflict or express a long-denied hurt can be a painful, difficult, and at the same time highly rewarding effort.

The chances are that the other person too would like to resolve the issue. Even if this isn't so, you will find that expressing *your* feelings—going more than halfway—will bring you a sense of personal satisfaction. You know you have done all *you* can to deal with the matter.

Risky, a little frightening perhaps, but then who will take the initiative and reach out if you don't?

10

Anger and Conflict—
Must They Be Aggressive?

Anger is a perfectly natural, useful human emotion. Everyone experiences it from time to time. What we each *do* with our anger is a different story. Non-assertive people often tell us, "I never get angry." We don't believe it! Everyone *feels* angry. Some people have so controlled themselves as to not openly *show* anger. Typically, such a controlled individual suffers from migraine headaches, asthma, ulcers, or skin problems.

We are convinced that expression of anger is a healthy thing, and that it can be done constructively. Persons who develop spontaneous assertiveness can express anger effectively in non-destructive ways, and thus preclude the necessity for aggressive actions.

As we have mentioned, an important step in non-destructive expression of anger is to *accept responsibility for your own feelings*. It is *you* who feel the anger, and that doesn't make the other person "stupid," an "S.O.B.," or the cause of your feeling.

A physical expression of strong feeling may be a good means for venting hostility. Banging the table, stomping the floor, crying, striking at the air, hitting a pillow are all non-destructive techniques for those who need physical release of strong feelings without aggression toward another person. (Note the caution about such forms of "release" discussed later in this chapter.)

Preventing the build-up of hostility over time by exercising spontaneous expression when you feel it is the healthiest way we know to deal with anger. Some of the verbal expressions often found useful include:

"I am very angry."	"I'm boiling mad."
"I am becoming very mad."	"I am extremely upset."
	"Stop bothering me."
"I strongly disagree with you."	"I think that's unfair."
	"Don't do that to me."
"I get damn mad when you say/do that."	"Cut it out."
"I am very disturbed/ distressed by this whole thing."	"You have no right to say/do that."
	"I really don't like that."
"It bothers me."	"That pisses me off."

All too often we have observed persons who express anger, frustration, or disappointment with another by cowardly, indirect, and unnecessarily hurtful methods. Moreover, if the desired goal is to change the behavior of the intended target, these approaches are rarely successful. A classic example is the case of the newlyweds, Martha and John. In the first few weeks of their marriage, Martha had discovered at least a dozen of John's habits which she found objectionable. Unfortunately for both, she was unable—or unwilling —to find the courage to confront John openly with her concerns. Instead she chose the "safe" way to express her dislike of John's behavior; she confided in her mother. Worse yet, not content with almost daily telephone conversations with her mother about John's shortcomings, she also used family get-togethers as an occasion to berate John before the rest of the family.

This "see-how-bad-he-is" style, relating to a third person (or persons) one's dislikes of another, can have disastrous effects upon a relationship. John feels hurt, embarrassed, and hostile about Martha's attacks upon him. He wishes she had chosen the privacy of their own relationship to tell him of her annoyances. Instead of being motivated to change his habits, he responds to her aggressive approach with bitterness and a resolve to strike back by intensifying the very behaviors she would have him change.

Had Martha chosen courageously to assert herself directly by telling John of her feelings, she would have created a good foundation for a cooperative effort in modifying John's behavior.

Another example will help clarify our point of view concerning the expression of anger:

A man took his car to a large repair shop for a several-hour repair job. The maintenance was done on a first-come, first-served basis. He arrived at 8 A.M., but told the manager he would pick the car up around 4:30 P.M. When he returned the following verbal interchange took place:

Customer: "Hi, my name is X and I'm here to pick up my car."

Manager (looking through his worksheets): "I'm sorry, sir, we haven't gotten to your car yet."

C: "Damn! That really makes me mad! This is first-come, first-served, and I was here at 8 A.M. What happened?"

M: "It was our mistake, we put it in the back and got busy and overlooked it."

C: "Well, that doesn't do me any good. It is an inconvenience for me to get my car in and leave it all day."

M: "I know that and I apologize. I promise to get

it done first thing in the morning if you want to bring it back."

At this point the customer could decide what his options are and choose accordingly. He could try to get the manager to have someone fix his car by working overtime; he could decide to take his car elsewhere; he could return the next day for the repair work; he could demand that the shop arrange to loan him another car while the work is being done.

Notice the anger expressed by the customer without being aggressive toward the manager. He was rightfully mad and told the manager so without downgrading him as a person. He might have responded aggressively:

"You can take that repair job and shove it," and stormed out; or said, "You damn S.O.B.s never do anything right around here. I demand that you fix my car right now."

Most likely either of these statements would inflame the manager and reduce your chances of getting good service now or in the future. The important thing is to express your angry feelings without hurting someone (including yourself) in the process.

Honest, spontaneous, "gut-level" assertive expression will help to prevent inappropriate and destructive anger. First, it will often achieve your goals at the outset. Even when assertion doesn't gain what you're after, however, it still prevents the anger you might have directed toward yourself if you had done nothing.

There is, unfortunately, a popular mythology which would have us believe that any form of *ventilation* of aggression, as long as it involves no physical harm to another person, is quite healthy. On the contrary, the simple fact, repeatedly demonstrated by reputable psychological research, is that violence *begets* violence. While the idea of encouraging such venting may well remove unhealthy inhibitions against self-expression, we urge you to avoid *the error of equating aggression with assertion.*

We emphatically disapprove of the theory, popular among some psychological faddists of the day, that one ought to express hostility in such direct fashions as standing nose-to-nose with your spouse and shouting obscenities at each other, or lashing your opponent with a foam rubber "bat" or pillows.

If we teach and encourage violent expression as a style, persons who learn that style are unlikely to confine it to the relative safety of their therapy group! Family fights conducted on such grounds may soon outgrow the "rules" and become full-scale violent brawls.

Psychologist Leonard Berkowitz, for example, has reported experimental studies which confirm our contention that there are non-violent methods of emotional release which contain the benefits but not the harmful effects of direct aggression. He suggests that a direct aggressive attack provokes additional aggression, both in the attacker and in the subject.

In one study, for instance, women who were insulted were permitted two styles of response. Group one was allowed to describe their angry feelings to the insulter (e.g., "That really makes me mad"). Group two women were given freedom to strike back and attack the insulter. After the experiment, women in the "feeling description" group (one) maintained less hostile feelings toward their insulter than did the women in group two who were permitted to attack directly.

Berkowitz concludes, and we heartily agree, that although persons may "feel better" after venting hostility aggressively, such reinforcement of destructive acts leads to further hurtful behavior. Assertive responses, on the other hand, can both effectively express your strong feelings *and* give the other person a chance to respond non-defensively—and perhaps even to change that behavior toward you which angered you in the first place!

Constructive Conflict Resolution

Like anger, conflict is an inevitable consequence of being human, whenever we are in close contact with other persons. Lovers, families, friends, co-workers, governments all know too well the power and pain of seemingly irreconcilable points of view.

Yet a good deal of work has been accomplished in recent years to develop effective methods of conflict resolution. Two areas in particular have received considerable attention: conflict in intimate relationships and conflict in organizational settings. It may or may not surprise you to learn that the findings about conflict are remarkably constant in both settings.

Brian and Ruby have been married ten years and are planning the annual family vacation. Brian has wanted for some time to rent a house at the beach, and plan no specific schedule. Ruby is determined to travel in New England and visit points of historic interest. She has an itinerary all planned. When they reach the time for the decision to be made . . .

Ellen Harwood is head of the marketing department and Richard Fredericks is head of research at ABC Industries. The annual budget is being prepared and Ellen and Richard both have proposals for major increases in the next year's program in their respective areas. The ABC budget will not accommodate both requests. When Richard and Ellen face each other across the table at the Executive Board meeting on the budget . . .

Ruby and Brian, Richard and Ellen represent countless people in situations where conflict is inevitable. Behavioral scientists who have worked in this field have arrived at a number of conclusions which will help in almost any conflict situation. Notice how closely the methods parallel the concepts of assertive behavior we have discussed.

Conflict resolution is facilitated:

(1) When the parties avoid an "I will win, and you will lose" stance. It is possible for all parties to win—at least in part—and no one *need* lose.

(2) When the parties have the same information about the problem. Remember that each of us hears information through our own set of filters. Be sure you check out the facts!

(3) When the basic goals of the parties are compatible (e.g., "to rest and relax on vacation," not "where we will go").

(4) When the parties are honest and direct with each other.

(5) When each party accepts responsibility for his/her own feelings.

(6) When each party is willing to confront and deal with the problem openly, rather than avoiding or hiding from it.

(7) When some system of exchange is adopted. Bargaining, *quid pro quo,* contract negotiation are the heart of conflict resolution. If we collaborate in an effort to solve the problem, and each gives something the other wants, we can very likely arrive at some form of mutually acceptable solution.

Conflict which has reached a point of strong angry feelings can be resolved only if those feelings are expressed honestly and openly. An assertive "I'm really angry about your unwillingness to see my point of view" can be the beginning of a constructive dialogue. A non-assertive "Let's forget it" avoidance of the problem or an aggressive "You stubborn S.O.B." is certain to leave both sides frustrated and unsatisfied.

Go ahead, get angry! But develop a positive, honest, assertive style for expressing it. You, and those around you, will appreciate it.

11

Assertive Behavior Situations: Personal Relationships

The examples in this and the next three chapters depict typical situations in which assertive behavior is called for, but which often cause difficulty for non-assertive or aggressive persons. Each situation is first presented, but without a response on the part of the principal "actor." Alternative responses are then described from which the actor may choose his behavior in the situation. Each alternative response may be characterized in the "non-assertive-aggressive-assertive" paradigm. Finally, we have presented our own comments which we hope will be helpful to you in your own growing assertiveness.

Each of the situations presented is designed for use as described in Chapter 7:

(1) Select a situation appropriate to your needs.

(2) Read the situation description, filling in such details as may be desired.

(3) Follow Steps 3 to 6 utilizing the alternative responses suggested here for the situation, as well as others you may think of.

(4) Enact the role-playing and feedback exercises described in Steps 7 to 10.

(5) Continue the remaining steps in the development of assertive behavior.

The chapters are grouped according to several characteristic types of situations: close-interpersonal, consumer, employment, school, and social. In each case only a few situations are suggested although the number of categories and examples is as infinite as life. In addition to this series of representative illustrations, one may on his own initiative apply assertive behavior to examples from his own life.

Close Interpersonal Relationships

Usually the most important area of assertion is interpersonal assertion because it concerns our behavior with those personally closest to us. Relationships between parent and child, husband and wife, brother and sister, brother and brother, or sister and sister are those we typically think of, but of course one can expand it to whatever extent is necessary. That is, depending on each person's individual situation, close interpersonal assertions might be between those engaged or living together under a variety of circumstances. The common factor we are speaking of here is a love feeling of some kind. Whether stated explicitly or not, there is a sense of mutual commitment. You feel that you have to "stay in there" and work harder to make things stay somewhat smooth between you. If your boss gives you a hard time at the office, theoretically you can quit; if the clerk gives you lousy service, you just don't go back; if a co-worker acts strange, you can choose to avoid him, and so on. But if something needs to be ironed out between us and those closest to us, this typically has our first priority. How many people come to a psychologist because they can't get along with their barber? On the other hand, we see a good many people heading for marriage counselors, sending their children to psychiatrists or becoming involved in therapies to overcome how they feel their parents adversely influenced them.

Close interpersonal assertions are especially difficult because we are typically overly concerned with not offending or hurting the feelings of our loved ones. Too often we act as if we had ESP because we believe we know how the other person feels or will feel about what we may say or do. Mind reading is bound to get you into a lot of trouble, especially when much of it is tied up in the past. There is no doubt about it that previous learning is a powerful thing; however, we usually go beyond the call of duty by being overly cautious and sensitive about the feelings of others.

Read the following situations, choose your response, then read the commentary that follows.

"SLUMBER PARTY"

Your twelve-year-old daughter is having a slumber party with five other girls. It is past 2 A.M. and the girls should have settled down to sleep by now, but they are still quite noisy.

Alternative Responses:

(1) You toss and turn in bed wishing your spouse would get up and say something to the girls. You do a slow burn, but just lie there trying to block out the sounds.

(2) Jumping out of bed, you thoroughly scold and berate the girls, especially your daughter, for unlady-like conduct.

(3) Talking to the girls in a tone which they will recognize as "meaning business," you tell them that

they have had enough fun for tonight. You point out that you need to arise early tomorrow, and that everyone needs to get to sleep.

Commentary:

(1) By putting off handling the situation you allow the anger feelings to build up inside you. This is not healthy mentally or physically for you. Try to assert yourself as soon as you feel angry about their noise bothering you. In addition, if the problem bothers you, handle it yourself. Don't allow or force others to assert themselves because of your feelings; take care of your own life. A final point concerns the fact of your being an excellent model for the girls if you do assert yourself.

(2) We believe that by age 12 you can treat children assertively. There is no need to scold or use words like "unladylike." These only serve to alienate you by embarrassing your daughter in front of her friends. Again, this is not being a good model.

(3) By appealing to the girls' sense of judgment, the effect they are having on others, you invite them to respond appropriately. If they pay little attention to your assertion, then tougher measures are in order; be sure you are not making idle threats. The important point is that if you are truly assertive, there will usually be no call for another round.

"LATE FOR DINNER"

Your husband was supposed to be home for dinner right after work. Instead, he returns hours later explaining he was out with the boys for a few drinks. He is somewhat tipsy.

Alternative Responses:

(1) You say nothing about how discourteous he has been to you, but simply start preparing something for him to eat.

(2) Screaming, yelling, or crying, you make the point very clear that you think he is a drunken fool who doesn't care about your feelings and is a poor example for the children. You ask him what the neighbors will think. You tell him he can get his own dinner.

(3) You calmly and steadfastly let him know that he should have informed you beforehand that he was going out for a few drinks and would likely be late. You inform him that his dinner is in the kitchen.

Commentary:

(1) We feel that you should express your feelings about his lateness, no matter whether he has done this before or not. Your saying nothing tells him it is okay, you don't mind, and that such behavior will be okay in the future.

(2) Screaming, yelling or crying, or calling him names does not solve your problem and only serves to place an extra burden on the person with whom you are trying to communicate. Additionally, to place interpretations on his actions (not caring for your feelings, etc.) is unfair of you based on one example. Keep your assertions simple and direct.

(3) Very good. You are dealing only with your feelings and express those in a calm but firm manner. There is no reason to yell or scream or cry because that truly does not make your message more effective.

"VISITING RELATIVE"

Aunt Margaret, with whom you prefer not to spend much time, is on the telephone. She has just told you of her plans to spend three weeks visiting you, beginning next week.

Alternative Responses:

(1) You think, "Oh, no!" but say, "We'd *love* to have you come and stay as long as you like."

(2) You tell her the children have just come down with bad colds, and the spare bed has a broken spring, and you'll be going to Cousin Bill's weekend after next—none of which is true.

(3) You say, "We'll be glad to have you come for the weekend, but we simply can't invite you for longer. A short visit is happier for everyone, and we'll want to see each other again sooner if we keep it brief."

Commentary:

(1) By thinking one thing and saying another you are being incongruent with yourself. When you are incongruent you are likely to come across falsely with others either by being overly sweet or the opposite, short-tempered and crabby. Most people see right through these responses and realize you have feelings

you are hiding. So you may as well speak your honest feelings in the first place.

(2) She probably will say she will bring along loads of Vitamin C, an extra spring for the bed, and that she hasn't seen Cousin Bill for years and would love to go along. Don't hint around, hoping someone will figure out what you mean, because—even if they figure it out—you will have hurt them much more than if you were honest in the first place.

(3) Assertiveness doesn't make you into a cold, cruel, hard person. As this response illustrates, you can compromise at times and make things better all the way around. Choice is the key. If you know you can assert yourself, you are able to be more flexible in life in situations such as these.

"PAST MIDNIGHT"

Your teenage son has just returned from a school party. It is 3 o'clock in the morning, and you have been frantic, concerned primarily for his well-being, since you had expected him home by midnight.

Alternative Responses:

(1) You turn over and go to sleep.

(2) You shout, "Where the hell have you been? Do you have any idea what time it is? You've kept me up all night! You thoughtless, inconsiderate, no-good bum, I ought to make you sleep in the street!"

(3) You say, "I have been very worried about you, son. You said you'd be home at midnight, and I have

been frantic for hours. Are you all right? I wish you had called me!"

Commentary:

(1) Going to sleep certainly doesn't solve the problem of all of the feelings you were experiencing about his lateness. Even if you are relieved that he is home, you should still find out what has happened and express your feelings assertively. If you respond by going to sleep, he will assume that what he did is fine for the future too.

(2) The problem with this response is that he may have a legitimate excuse so that your outburst would be unwarranted. Even if he was late for reasons unacceptable to you, you still need to establish communication. Your response doesn't allow him to express his real feelings. We want you to express your feelings, but do so constructively rather than destructively. With an aggressive response you may obtain obedience to your wishes, but you usually sacrifice a good self-concept in your son and genuine communication between you.

(3) Good. Don't be afraid to show your concern about his welfare, but at the same time to question what held him up. It is his responsibility to keep you informed when he is unable to keep the agreed-upon time deadline.

12

Does Assertiveness Have a Place on the Job?

Work. The American Way. The "source of a man's dignity." The tools one uses to change the world. "Find a job in which you are *fulfilled*," parents and guidance counselors tell countless youngsters every day. Don't have just a *job*, have a *career!*

Such are the ways we have glorified the labors by which we maintain ourselves in the world. Yet Warnath remains true to the *real* world. Studs Terkel, in his monumental book *Working*, confirms what Warnath theorizes: people are largely dissatisfied with the lack of influence they have on the job, with their limited personal rewards from work, with the absence of value to be derived from their efforts.

It has become clear that, vocational theorists and social planners notwithstanding, most of us do not find much self-fulfillment in our work. In an increasingly production-and-profit-oriented world of work, industrial technology has developed greater "efficiency" by specialization and routine. It's pretty hard to find much job satisfaction in repeatedly performing a highly routine chore.

It is interesting to note that a recent study of the job market in Japan reveals the prevalence there of similar attitudes. Across the world students have voiced their strong feelings against what they believe to be an "elitist" system of steps from school to university to jobs. Yet these same individuals, when they enter the job market, find themselves conforming to the depersonalizing demands of a system which rewards conformity and non-assertion.

As we discussed in Chapter 1, personal powerlessness is pervasive, and it can be devastating to the individual. Yet as we have seen throughout this book, there are ways of expressing yourself, of having influence, of doing something about your situation. These methods are as useful on the job as anywhere else.

Sure, you may not change the world, or even the office or plant, but you *can* maintain your own dignity and integrity. You *can* prevent or remedy the "little murders" which are an ever-present threat to your self-respect. You can be an assertive worker *and* keep your job. You can be an assertive supervisor, meet your quotas, *and* have a happier staff.

We have found that assertive behavior is being encouraged, trained, and rewarded in a wide variety of industrial settings. Personnel development programs in banks, oil companies, insurance companies, publishing and broadcast media, architectural firms, government organizations, and many others are including assertion training. The message we are hearing is that, when supervisors and employees treat each other with mutual respect, acting assertively toward each other in *both* directions, morale and production are higher.

There are risks, of course. Indeed, we know a young woman, Kathy, who risked—and lost—a $1,000-a-month job because she asserted herself. Her supervisor had been treating her unfairly and she spoke up about it—assertively—but he was unable to handle her expression of her feelings, and fired her. Kathy had decided in advance that she was willing to take the risk. Unfortunately, her supervisor was one of those who would not accept an assertive response. In our observation, this is a rare occurrence. Most supervisors respect their staff members who are willing to keep relationships honest, to speak up when they agree or disagree—as long as the employee handles the situation assertively. That is, when the worker adopts an expressive position, takes responsibility for his/her own feelings, and does not demean or gossip about others in the process.

Similarly, employees respect and work hard for the assertive supervisor, who does not use put-down tactics in criticizing, who is as free with praise as with criticism, who treats an employee as a valuable human being without patronizing. So often we find bosses whose personal insecurity leads them to assume a superior/distant/dominant attitude over their staff members—as you will see when you meet Wayne in Chapter 17. Such people are afraid that if they don't utilize "top sergeant" tactics, their employees will not respect (and thereby work hard for) them. So much energy and human potential are wasted in such departments!

If you are in a management role and find conflict to be a major concern, you may wish to review Chapter 10, in particular the discussion of application of the concepts of assertiveness to conflict resolution.

Now let us analyze examples from this area.

Employment Situations

"WORKING LATE"

You and your spouse have an evening engagement which has been planned for several weeks. Today is the date and you plan to leave immediately after work. During the day, however, your supervisor indicates that she/he would like you to stay late this evening to work on a special assignment.

Alternative Responses:

(1) You say nothing about your important plans and simply agree to stay until the work is finished.

(2) In a nervous, abrupt voice you say, "No, I will not work late tonight." Then you criticize the boss for not planning the work schedule better. You then turn back to the work you were doing.

(3) Talking to the supervisor in a firm but pleasant voice, you tell of your important plans and say you will not be able to stay this evening to work on the special assignment.

Commentary:

(1) If you chose this approach you are in double trouble, first with yourself, second with your spouse. Your spouse has a perfect right to be upset at your non-assertiveness, your inability to speak for yourself and for what is important to you. So often we hear complaints like "Oh, if I say anything to the boss I'll get fired, I just know I will" or "The boss is just not capable of understanding my viewpoint." Don't be a mind reader or a fortune teller, be assertive.

(2) This response is giving yourself away on several counts. First, if your voice is nervous and abrupt it signals the other person to beef up their defenses. Then, if you criticize the boss by making a value judgment on how the schedules are made out, there will be more bristling on his/her part. Stick with the

fact that you have already made plans and that they are important. Don't allow yourself to get sidetracked by criticizing. Even if your claim is legitimate it is better to go in some other time and discuss that matter specifically.

(3) The choice here is a good assertive response. Your voice is firm without calling for the other person to retaliate. You clearly state your case and don't hedge by asking, "Do you think I should work anyway?"

"JOB ERROR"

You have made a mistake on some aspect of your job. Your supervisor discovers it and is letting you know rather harshly that you should not have been so careless.

Alternative Responses:

(1) Overapologizing, you say you are sorry, you were stupid, how silly of you, you'll never let it happen again.

(2) You bristle up and say that he has no business whatsoever criticizing your work. You tell him/her to leave you alone and not bother you in the future because you are capable of handling your own work.

(3) You agree that you made the mistake, say you are sorry and will be more careful next time. You add that you feel she/he is being somewhat harsh and you see no need for that.

Commentary:

(1) When you react in this way, by putting yourself down, you are giving the other permission to treat you the same way in the future. If others do not know your true feelings they have no reason to change their response to you.

(2) By reacting in this manner you most likely provoke him/her to further harshness with you. By being combative you will not solve your problem; you'll only worsen it. Even though she/he has treated you harshly, the best response is still not to return his/her harshness, but rather to be assertive.

(3) The boss does have the right to criticize your work, but there is no need for harshness. Also, there is nothing wrong with admitting to mistakes. This does not make you appear to be a weak person whereas denying it might.

"TARDY"

One of your subordinates has been coming in late consistently for the last three or four days.

Alternative Responses:

(1) You grumble to yourself or to others about the situation, but say nothing to the person, hoping he/she will start coming in early.

(2) You tell the worker off, indicating that he/she has no right to take advantage of you and that he/she had better get to work on time or else you will see that he/she is fired.

(3) Approaching the worker, you point out that you have observed him/her coming in late recently and wonder if there is an explanation. If he/she does not have a legitimate excuse, you say firmly that he/she should start coming to work on time. If the excuse seems legitimate, you still say that he/she should have come to you and explained the situation rather than saying nothing at all, leaving you "up in the air."

Commentary:

(1) Most of us spend too much time talking to ourselves and others about problems we are having with another person. We spend our time grumbling and gossiping instead of taking positive steps to remedy the problem.

(2) Here we see a classic response of not keeping your life clear. As soon as it begins to bother you that the worker is coming in late, it is your responsibility to handle it then. By waiting, you allow the steam inside you to elevate your aggression quotient.

(3) Concern about your employee is shown by first trying to find out whether or not there is a legitimate problem. The response here allows you to assert yourself in either case because, even if there was a good excuse, the employee is still responsible for keeping you posted.

"JOB INTERVIEW"

You are in a job interview, and you can tell that the interviewer is about to wrap up the interview without giving you a chance to have some of your concerns about the job answered. He/she has just said, "Well, I guess that's it. I'll let you know what we decide about you."

Alternative Responses:

(1) You start to say something several times, but your heart begins to beat so fast you feel too nervous to say anything.

(2) You ask, "Are you done now? Because I have a say-so in this job situation too." You tell the person that they are not just picking you; you have to approve of their company also. Then you proceed to tell him/her in an obviously bragging manner how great you are and that you'll have to have more money.

(3) You say, "Before we finish today I wonder if you could answer some important questions I have about the job?" He says, "Certainly." Then you say, "I also would like to expand on some of my background that was contained in the application form." Proceeding, you clearly state your concerns and views without being pushy. At the end you ask how soon you can expect a response from him.

Commentary:

(1) If you don't speak up for yourself, no one else will, especially in this type of situation. We don't want you to be pushy, but when you first have feelings you want to say something, do so. If you speak when you feel the urge, instead of "being polite" and putting it off, chances are your heart won't beat so fast. Thinking too much about what you'll say, repeating it many times in your mind, does build anxiety.

(2) Maybe if you are the son/daughter of the company's owner, you will be able to get away with this response. We would imagine that the interviewer would feel that you wouldn't fit in too well on the job, however. If you present yourself assertively, you can talk about your good points without being overbearing.

(3) Very good! By putting forth the best that you know, you increase your chances for securing the job. We don't mean that you should be false, but only that you don't hide your good qualities behind timidness or bravado. Employers are not looking for "yes" men or women who only echo what they say. They are after those who are self-confident and able to speak up without offending others.

13 _____

Assertiveness in Social Situations

There is a distinct relationship between feeling good about oneself and assertion. As we have told you, your self-confidence and therefore your self-concept are going to change for the better the more you are able to be assertive. In essence, one can be friendlier with oneself. And there is another vital relationship involved in learning to be assertive also: that of feeling good about or liking others. Being able to be a good friend to yourself frees you to be friendlier with others, which in turn leads to being a good friend to others. As one of our clients put it, "I can like other people now; I don't have to be afraid of or hate them any more."

It is so important to be friendly and have friends in life. Why else are we here? Everything we do seems to revolve around other people, and much of the time this is in a social context. So shouldn't we be able to be at ease when we meet a stranger, or get together in groups, or when we are involved in dating relationships? If one were truly assertive, would there ever be a need to be afraid of any social situation?

Please read and respond to the following questions:

Social Situations

"BREAKING THE ICE"

At a party where you don't know anyone except the host, you want to circulate and get to know others. You walk up to three people who are conversing.

Alternative Responses:

(1) You stand close to them and smile but say nothing, waiting for them to notice you.

(2) You listen to the subject they are talking about, then break in and state that you disagree with someone's viewpoint.

(3) You wait for a pause in the conversation and then introduce yourself and ask if you may join in.

Commentary:

(1) At times when you approach a small group this way, someone will notice your smile and standing close and will be kind enough to help you out by inviting you into the group. Wouldn't it be much better to be more in control of your own destiny, though? If you sit back and wait, you might end up waiting for an extended period of time.

(2) This is considered an aggressive response because it involves breaking in while they are talking. This will usually offend the person speaking. Disagreeing with someone's viewpoint is okay—as long as you do so assertively without having to interrupt.

(3) This is fine. However, be careful that you aren't waiting for an extended period of time for a pause. Another good technique is to listen to the conversation and ask a question or make a point about the topic. Then later you might introduce yourself if that seems appropriate at the time.

"MAKING A DATE"

You are interested in a date with a person of the opposite sex whom you have met and talked with three or four times recently.

Alternative Responses:

(1) You sit around the telephone rehearsing in your mind what you will say and how your friend will respond. Several times you lift the phone and are almost finished dialing, then hang up.

(2) You phone and as soon as your friend answers you respond by saying, "Hi, baby, we're going out together this weekend." Seemingly taken aback, your friend asks who is calling.

(3) You call and when your friend answers, you ask how school (job, etc.) is going. The reply is, "Fine, except I am worried about a test I will be taking soon." Following the lead, you talk for a few minutes about the test. Then you say that there is a show downtown this Friday evening and that you would like it if the two of you would go together.

Commentary:

(1) It does take action to get results. Even response

(2) is better than doing nothing at all. Trial and error is the best way to learn. Never let mistakes stop you either; simply analyze what happened and try again.

(2) Slow down a little; don't be so pushy. Perhaps you are God's gift to the opposite sex, but you come on too strong. Even if the person responds, beware, because she/he may be unable to say no. We have found that the best relationships between couples take place when both partners are assertive.

(3) Listening is a skill worth developing. In this case it was good to pick up the lead and talk about what is on the person's mind. Also, we feel it is a good idea to state what you have in mind for the evening, then ask them out, rather than saying generally, "Are you free Friday night?" Also, don't say, "Are you busy this weekend?" Be more specific; this allows the other person to feel less pressured.

"THE INTRODUCTION"

You are engaged in a conversation with a friend, Sherrie, when another friend, Tom, comes into the room. Your two friends do not know each other. Tom sees you, walks over smiling, and starts talking to you. Sherrie remains silent.

Alternative Responses:

(1) Several times during the conversation you think about introducing your two friends. Tom keeps looking over at Sherrie and smiling.

(2) With a frown on your face you say to Tom, "Since you're here, I guess I should introduce you two."

(3) After exchanging greetings with Tom, you say, "Let me introduce you two. Tom, this is Sherrie." Then you say a few words about whatever background information is pertinent to the situation. That is, you could say, "Sherrie works in (one department or section of the building) and Tom in (another)."

Commentary:

(1) Whatever your reason is for not introducing your two friends, it can't be a good one. If you can't think of someone's name or exact job title, say so. Highly formal introductions aren't really necessary, either. Introducing them in some manner will prevent you from putting yourself down later for not having tried some approach.

(2) This is a double put-down. First, your non-verbal response doesn't go unnoticed, and second, your verbal response is a put-down by using the words "since" and "guess."

(3) It helps to go beyond simply giving first names. Helping them get over what may be an awkward moment is insured with this response. You should also be ready to help them out during this conversation. Don't simply give them a little background information and then remain silent. Join in with them.

"NEW IN THE NEIGHBORHOOD"

You have recently moved into a neighborhood where you know no one. You would like to be friendly and get to know those close by.

Alternative Responses:

(1) During the time you are home, you wonder why no one comes over to say hello or at least to borrow something. Several of the neighbors have smiled at you or waved to you, but no one has come to talk. "What's wrong with them?" you think. "Why aren't they friendly?"

(2) After a week or so you decide that they are all a bunch of fools. "Don't they have more sense than to avoid me?" you think. You decide to "show them" and start ignoring any little smile or wave that comes your way.

(3) If any of the neighbors smiles or waves to you, you approach them and introduce yourself. If no one shows any signs of friendliness, you find a good time to approach them anyway, introduce yourself, chat for a while, and maybe invite them to come over for coffee sometime.

Commentary:

(1) Don't think that there is something wrong with them or with yourself because they don't come over. Simply act on your own wishes to get to know them and go introduce yourself. If your manners dictate that they should introduce themselves to you because they were there first, forget your manners and do it anyway.

(2) By doing this you will only isolate yourself further. This is also considered an aggressive response because of your attitude toward them. Remember, if you can only learn to be assertive, you won't have to be hostile and dislike others.

(3) Right. There is nothing wrong with taking responsibility to get to know them. Ann Landers, or whoever, will forgive you. Why sit around and suffer, when you can be living an active life?

14

Consumer Situations and Self-Assertion

The marketplace is a virtual battleground for large numbers of people. From complaints about auto repairs to arguments with landlords over security deposits to hassles with the bank over checking accounts, there are thousands of situations in the consumer world to cause upset if we don't know how to handle them successfully. Ralph Nader and his raiders and other consumer protection agencies have helped make life easier for us. Columns in newspapers and magazines continually give us hints about what to do if we feel we have been taken advantage of or to avoid being taken advantage of financially or otherwise. Most of these sources miss the important ingredient, however— the interpersonal one.

We feel, and we have evidence to support, that by learning to be assertive we can eliminate a great many of the consumer complaints. Small claims courts are loaded with cases dealing with conflicts over money. Many of these could be avoided completely if we knew how to apply the basic principles of assertion. Much of a lawyer's time is spent in dealing with situations that could be dealt with by the individuals involved if they would practice being assertive.

By being assertive you can learn how to handle line jumpers in the grocery store or elsewhere, how to return faulty items of merchandise, how to get your meals prepared as you ordered them, and so on. Think of the time, money, and turmoil this can save. By being assertive you do not allow yourself to be a consumer victim. You learn to be in charge of your own destiny when dealing with the world of goods and services.

We are not implying that those in charge of the market world are out to get us. There seems to be ample evidence, though, that if you act like an easy mark you will be treated that way. On the other hand, as often as not in the salesworld the person who is too pushy as a consumer will be rewarded. As we've stressed before, however, overall, the pitfalls of being aggressive are not worth a few successes. Feeling guilty later for hurting a clerk's feelings, or those of another customer, is only one of the prices we pay for being too abrasive. In general, however, the people we meet in the consumer world are not setting out consciously to take advantage of us.

Actually, in addition to utilizing assertive training programs to improve employee-employer relationships (Chapter 13), employers should also be training their workers who deal with the public. Too often we have observed sales personnel mishandling consumers by coming across either non-assertively or too aggressively. A great deal of money could be saved, either directly or indirectly, through good assertive public relations.

Read the following examples from the consumer marketplace and select your responses.

Consumer Situations

"HAIRCUT"

At the barber shop, the barber has just finished cutting your hair and turns the chair toward the mirror so you can inspect. You feel that you would like the sides trimmed more.

Alternative Responses:

(1) You either nod your head in assent or say, "That's okay," or say nothing.

(2) You state abruptly that he should have done a more thorough job or say sarcastically, "You sure didn't take much off the sides, did you?"

(3) You point out that you would like to have the sides trimmed more and ask the barber to do so.

Commentary:

(1) A response like this means that you held your feelings inside. These feelings are very likely to come out in some form later. Often a series of situations like this may happen over a short period of time. Eventually the pressure builds up to such an extent that you take it out on yourself or others.

(2) By coming across with abruptness and sarcasm you are offending the other person. This usually can be prevented if you will speak your feelings as soon as you recognize them. Although he/she will probably understand your intended meaning, we would rather have you be more direct. Instead of stating the fact that he/she didn't take much off, say what you want to see take place.

(3) This is good because the reason you are turned toward the mirror in the first place is to give you the opportunity to give the barber feedback on the job.

Even if your hair has been cut too short, you should speak your feelings in order that the problem may be remedied the next time or for the next person.

"SHORTCHANGED"

As you are leaving a store after purchasing some item, you discover that you have been shortchanged by 70 cents.

Alternative Responses:

(1) Pausing for a moment, you try to decide if 70 cents is worth the effort. After a few moments, you decide it is not and go on your way.

(2) You hurry back in the store and loudly demand that you receive back your 70 cents, making a derogatory comment about "cashiers who can't add."

(3) Reentering the store, you catch the attention of the clerk, saying that you believe you were short-changed by 70 cents. In the process of explaining, you display the change you received back.

Commentary:

(1) Try not to talk yourself out of your feelings. Your response of pausing and trying to decide if it is worth the effort to return usually means that it is. Trust your first impulse as long as it is not a destructive one.

(2) If you were the cashier and had made the mistake, would you appreciate having someone "loudly demand" or say "cashiers who can't add"? You can

accomplish your goal without putting down the other person.

(3) The best approach is given here. Displaying the change returned to you is especially important, as is returning immediately. Waiting a week would "throw off" the clerk because he wouldn't remember.

"WAITING IN LINE"

You are standing near a cash register waiting to pay for your purchase and have it wrapped. Others, who came after you, are being waited on first. You are getting tired of waiting.

Alternative Responses:

(1) You either take the article back to where you picked it up or edge closer trying to catch the eye of the clerk.

(2) Shouting that you sure get poor service in this store, you slam the intended purchase down on the counter and walk out of the store.

(3) In a voice loud enough to be heard, you tell the clerk you were ahead of people who had already been waited upon. Further state that you would like to be waited on now.

Commentary:

(1) We assume that the item and your time are valuable to you, so taking it back only serves to frustrate you further. Trying to edge closer to gain the attention of the clerk is likely to be more frustrating

also. Typically, clerks are too busy to monitor the line so they simply serve the closest customers, not worrying about where they came from.

(2) This combination is aggressive plus non-assertive. Shouting that "you sure get poor service" most likely would surprise the clerk because chances are the clerk did not notice your dilemma. If you walk out without explaining, you neither get to make your purchase nor let the clerk know exactly what was happening with the line.

(3) Assertion relies on the fact that most people react sensibly when a problem is pointed out to them assertively. By this response you are almost assured of getting the line straightened up and yourself waited on in turn.

"AUTOMOBILE WOES"

You've noticed a strange clacking noise coming from your car engine in the last day or two and decide to take it in for a check-up and repair job. You've had problems with car repair establishments before. After hearing your story, the repairman says, "It'll need some work on that engine; do you want us to go ahead and fix it?"

Alternative Responses:

(1) You feel reluctant to answer since you've been "ripped off" before, but you know the work needs to be done so you say, "Oh well, go ahead."

(2) Snapping back and pointing your finger at him, you say, "I know how you hot dogs *fix* things. Now

you listen to me. I want this G-- D--- car opened up
and analyzed and you, *you* call me before you make
one little move to fix it."

(3) You indicate that you're not sure, because
working on the engine could end up in a lot of money. You tell him you'd like him to open it up, analyze
what needs to be done, write up an itemized estimate
which would include work to be done and total cost.
Before you leave, be sure he agrees not to start work
until you sign the estimate, of which you get a copy.

Commentary:

(1) It is so important to say your feelings. If you
have been taken advantage of before, you should say
so even if this isn't the repair shop that did the job
previously. Also, by simply saying "go ahead," you
leave yourself wide open for all sorts of repair work.

(2) Even though you may successfully get your
wishes by reacting this way, you are likely to suffer
later. Typically, an aggressive outburst will leave you
feeling guilty and physically let down. Some people
even tremble, have an upset stomach or a headache,
feel shaky, and so on after the conflict is over.

(3) This is the best way to approach the problem
in order to protect yourself. Consumer protection
agencies recommend this approach, which goes along
well with being assertive.

15

School Situations

It is generally accepted that those learners who assertively participate gain the most in their learning experience.

Sitting in class like a bump on a log usually fosters boredom, confusion, and even falling asleep. On the other hand, if you come on too strong by endless talking, by continually putting the teacher on the spot with impossible questions or by railroading your classmates when you work together on projects, your learning experience will also be less than rewarding. Assertive training has been highly valuable in helping students raise questions in class, make presentations and reports, respond to teacher questions, express opinions, and participate in group discussions. This applies whether one is approaching the learning experience from an aggressive or non-assertive angle.

Although the title of this section is *School Situations*, the principles stressed are the same for community meetings and lectures of various kinds (e.g., PTA, City Council, school board, religious group meetings); for conversations around the dinner table or at parties; for any situation where it is important to express yourself about your knowledge or to gain more from someone else's knowledge.

Read the following situations and apply the examples to make learning a lifelong event alive with enthusiasm.

School Situations

"QUIET PROF"

You are in a physics lecture with 300 students. The professor speaks softly and you know that many others are having the same trouble as yourself in hearing him.

Alternative Responses:

(1) You continue to strain to hear, eventually move close to the front of the room, but say nothing about his too-soft voice.

(2) You yell out, "Speak up!"

(3) You raise your hand, get the professor's attention, and ask if he would mind speaking louder.

Commentary:

(1) The difficulty with this response is that even if you can hear upon moving closer, there is a good chance many others cannot hear her/him too. We would suggest that you help the others out by speaking out about the problem. Another potential problem is that you still may not be able to hear when you move closer.

(2) By yelling out like this, you are choosing a response which is frustrating to the speaker. When you are giving a presentation, it is disconcerting to have someone blurt out in this manner. Also, you may find

that the lecturer does nothing about improving his/her volume when you use a basically anonymous response as you've done here.

(3) Yes, simply assume she/he does not realize that many cannot hear. Usually an individual who is speaking feels that their material is important and wants to ensure that all can hear. Additionally, they like to keep good rapport between themselves and the audience so that they usually accommodate appropriately made requests.

"CLARIFICATION"

In an English class, the teacher is discussing the contributions of classical language to modern English. You are puzzled by several of the references, and believe she/he has misstated an important concept.

Alternative Responses:

(1) You say nothing, but continue to puzzle over the concept, looking up another source at the library later in the day.

(2) You interrupt, telling him he has made an error, pointing out the mistake and correcting him from your own knowledge of the subject. Your tone and choice of words make him look somewhat ill-at-ease.

(3) You ask the teacher to further explain the concept, expressing your confusion and noting the source of your conflicting information.

Commentary:

(1) By asking in class you will most likely save yourself a good deal of study time. Also, by voicing your puzzlement you are expressing your feelings rather than holding them inside. Your speaking up will potentially help the teacher too, since he/she may indeed be confused.

(2) It is not necessary to interrupt in order to state your point. By raising your hand and gaining the instructor's attention, you will be less offensive in your approach. We feel it is better to state your concerns first and let the person discuss them than to state or imply that there has definitely been an error. By not overwhelming the person with words and voice tone the problem can be resolved more quickly.

(3) This is a very good way to handle the situation because you have included all of your concerns. The teacher does not have to feel defensive when you approach the problem in this way. Note that you are still being honest with your feelings, but that you are not "putting yourself upon" the teacher.

"MORALS"

You are one of eleven students in a psychology group discussion on human sexuality. The concepts being supported by three or four of the more verbal students are contrary to your personal moral code.

Alternate Responses:

(1) You listen quietly, not disagreeing openly with the other members or describing your own views.

(2) You loudly denounce the views which have

been expressed. Your defense of your own belief is strong, and you urge others to accept your point of view as the only correct one.

(3) You speak up in support of your own beliefs, identifying yourself with an apparently unpopular position, but not disparaging the beliefs of others in the group.

Commentary:

(1) When you keep quiet like this you deny yourself as a person. It is your right to speak your feelings even though you may be outnumbered. You will also usually be stimulating others to consider other viewpoints which otherwise they would not be aware of.

(2) When you speak in this manner you will turn off those sharing the opposite view and maybe even all the rest of the class. When you overwhelm people they typically shut you off, even if you may be 100 per cent correct. If your views are truly worth hearing, you should ensure they are heard.

(3) Great. At times in life we have to be courageous. This, of course, is not easy, but we have to risk being criticized, and maybe disliked, at times. The more we can avoid a "better than thou" attitude, the better all will feel.

"SMOKE GETS IN YOUR LUNGS"

You are at a public meeting in a large room. A man enters the room and sits down next to you, puffing enthusiastically on a large cigar. The smoke is very offensive to you.

Alternative Responses:

(1) You suffer the offensive smoke in silence, deciding it is the right of the other person to smoke if he wishes.

(2) You become very angry, demand that he move or put out the cigar, and loudly assail the evils and health hazards of the smoking habit.

(3) You firmly but politely ask him to refrain from smoking because it is offensive to you, or to sit in another seat if he prefers to continue smoking.

Commentary:

(1) We believe that it is better to let the person know how you feel about the smoke and then let them *choose* what to do. By suffering in silence you are assuming too much for the other person. If they are not informed of your feelings there is no way they can decide to give up their right to smoke.

(2) Often, if you will try assertion first, an angry response such as this will not be necessary. By demanding that he move and put out the cigar, you are denying him his right of choice. If you approach the problem assertively, most people are able to respond in a reasonable manner. Finally, you can be assertive in this instance without "blaring out" the ills of smoking.

(3) Yes, we believe that politeness, but assertively stated, is the best choice here. There is no need to muster up your forces to do battle before you have tried the peaceful, and yet firm, approach.

16 _____

How To Handle Put-Downs

Put-down behavior is a type of behavior that frequently occurs in our society. If it isn't someone else putting us down, we put ourselves down. Although it is difficult to categorize, there seem to be two basic areas of put-down behavior. The area of *general put-downs* includes everything that is not related to a specific grouping of traits one possesses. The area of *minority put-downs* is concerned with groupings of people who possess traits or characteristics which certain others have traditionally found to be different or offensive.

Some examples of the general put-down category are: being put down for not wearing a tie to work, for accidentally hitting a car or making a mistake, for not understanding a point someone is trying to explain, and so on. The minority put-down area has a multitude of subgroups within it such as blacks, Chicanos, Indians and other ethnic groups, prisoners, the mentally ill, women, the physically handicapped, obese people, children, left-handed people, short people, beautiful women or handsome men, senior citizens, alcoholics, rich people, poor people, and so on. Obviously, in some of these subgroups, such as ethnic and women, put-downs appear to be much more serious, complicated, and frequent than others, but it is almost impossible to scale the entire category further.

Put-downs from others and from ourselves can be

further categorized in terms of non-assertive and aggressive acts, as the verbally aggressive put-down; the non-verbal aggressive put-down; the verbally non-assertive put-down; and the non-verbal non-assertive put-down. The put-downs received from one's self may be classified as either covert put-downs or overt put-downs. First, we'll deal with put-downs from others.

The Verbally Aggressive Put-Down

This type of put-down is easy to identify because it is a blatant, direct, on-target response from someone. As you are aware, many put-downs are rather subtle and devious, but not this one. If you are being put down verbally in an aggressive manner, there is no mistaking the intent behind the message. Let us analyze an example to help clarify.

You are backing out of your parking lot space where the cars are jammed quite close together. While trying to maneuver, you accidentally hit and dent the side of a nearby car. As you get out to see how much damage you've done, the owner runs up yelling, "Hey, stupid! What the hell are you doing? I put a lot of money into my car and here I have to get into a parking lot near an idiot like you!"

We could alter the above situation to fit the Minority Put-Down category simply by having the receiver of the put-down comments be a black person. The comments would be changed to read something like, "Damn, are you niggers stupid!" and "You black S.O.B.!"

In either case, it isn't very difficult to figure out that you've been put down, is it? But what should you do now, how do you answer? We have found that the most important first step is to let the other person "run down" before you try to say anything. If you try to get a point in before the brunt of their outburst is dissipated, you may be in further trouble. So when you've decided they are ready to listen, you might say, "Listen, I am sorry I hit your car. I know you are very upset, but I didn't hit it on purpose. I don't mind your being mad, but I don't appreciate your calling me names. Now let me write down my insurance agent's address for you."

For the Minority Put-Down, we would follow along similar lines: "Listen, I hit your car, I know you're mad, I apologize. But it makes me mad when you call me 'nigger' and that stuff. That has nothing to do with my hitting your car, so cut it out. Now let me write down my insurance agent's address for you."

Your non-verbal response in the above situation will depend on how you feel inside. Chances are, you will feel the adrenalin pumping and find yourself very upset by the inflammatory comments of this person.

We feel that it is perfectly all right to show your anger by such things as (1) talking quickly and firmly, (2) holding your hand up like a stop sign when you say "listen," and (3) being soberly unsmiling. Notice that we didn't tell you to yell and cuss, or otherwise to return the other person's aggression. Chances are that you will feel aggressive in return, but nothing will be solved by venting your aggressive feelings. As long as you can be assertive, it won't hurt you to swallow an impulse to blast back. The four important elements of this response are: (1) apologize if you are wrong, even if you've just been downed; (2) recognize the other person's feelings ("I know you are upset")— this shows concern and that, since you know, they don't have to repeat it for you again; (3) tell him/her your feelings about the derogatory comments; (4) suggest a solution which is merited, based on the problem, and tends to close the discussion.

The Non-Verbal Aggressive Put-Down

In this situation, we find it is less obvious that we are being put down because no words are spoken. However, there are readily observable, non-verbal cues: a hard, glaring stare, a hands-on-hips rigid stance, a doubled-up fist being shaken at you, or a hard aggressive walk, and so on. This area is difficult to isolate as a category by itself because words usually burst out along with the non-verbal response or shortly thereafter. Let us look at one example, however. This example from the General Put-Down category comes from a marital situation reenacted in a therapist's office.

Him: "You always say that to me, and when I tell you it isn't true and I can back it up, you don't listen."

Her: (Halfway through his response, she tosses her head back as if struck by a blow.)

As soon as the husband has completed his sentence, the therapist points out her non-verbal response and checks their reactions. Typically, he would be aware of it, but will have said nothing, and she would not. She should be encouraged to say words rather than to give out signals which can easily be misinterpreted without the truth ever coming out in the open. If he discovers her head toss on his own, he should give a response such as:

Him (stopping his talk): "Do you know what you just did?" *or* "I would appreciate it if you wouldn't toss your head while I'm talking."

Her: "What do you mean?"

Him: "Well, when I said, 'You always say that to me,' you tossed your head. That really bothers me because I don't know what to think of it. Could you wait until I finish my point, then say how you're feeling, rather than doing that?"

Her: "I'll try. I guess you made me mad, but I see what you mean about telling you."

The two most important considerations in this example are: *first*, that he doesn't *interpret* her severe toss of the head, but simply points out that it bothers him; and *second*, that he doesn't put off his feelings, he speaks about the problem as soon as he recognizes it within himself.

The Verbally Non-Assertive Put-Down

In comparison to the verbally aggressive put-down, this put-down is much harder to figure out. Exactly what the other person is trying to tell you is confusing because it is said so subtly and indirectly.

EXAMPLE: GENERAL PUT-DOWN

You have recently separated from your spouse and are dating someone much younger than yourself and all of your relatives know about it. One day while at a family gathering, your aunt walks up with a big smile and says, "Hi there, still robbing the cradle?" Not catching what she means, you say, "What do you mean?" Her reply is, "Oh, you know, all the fun you are having with those young kids, going out and all." Immediately she adds, "Well, nice seeing you. I've got to rush," after which she scurries away to talk to someone else.

EXAMPLE: MINORITY PUT-DOWN

You are Chicano and are attending a mainly Anglo party made up of your co-workers. Your supervisor, an Anglo, comes over and is chit-chatting to a small group of you and your friends. The supervisor, Jack, is trying to figure out what music and games will take place at the party and turns to you with a big smile and says, "And you, Maria, of course, can play and strum the guitar for us. You people have a lot of musical ability." Jack's tone is definitely condescending.

Obviously, once you figure it out, you realize you are being put down and in a backhanded manner.

In each example, they certainly aren't speaking their feelings directly. The aunt will not even take responsibility for her feelings, but hurries off. Neither faced you alone, but chose the protection of a group situation.

Certainly these situations are not easy to resolve. We all know of people who haven't spoken to each other for years because of similar incidents. Perhaps our first tendency is to avoid any further encounter with persons such as the aunt or Jack, to write them off as busybodies or bigots. The trouble with such a choice is that it does not resolve your feelings or theirs. There is a gap between you, the air is heavy or your relationship clouded. Even if they did not make you mad, did not hurt your feelings at all, we still think you need to have a talk with them about their response to you. The reason for this is that from their viewpoint the air is still not clear. Of course, you could say that it is their problem, not yours, but our feeling is that the best alternative is to handle the situation instead of avoiding it. If you don't approach them, they may even do the same thing to you again, so it is best to deal with the situation promptly.

The question remains, though, how shall you approach your aunt or supervisor? Let's take the aunt first. Plan to set up an opportunity to be alone with her as soon as possible after the first encounter. However, don't follow her right after her put-down of you and confront her. You could approach her later at the gathering or within the next few days and say, "Could I speak to you alone for a few minutes?"

Then the sequence might proceed as follows:

Aunt: "Oh, what about?"

You: "Something you said earlier bothered me and I would like to clear it up."

Aunt: "I was just teasing, don't take anything I say seriously."

You: "I'd still like to talk; can we go?"
(Outside)

You: "Perhaps you were teasing earlier, but it really bothered me the way you came across. I felt like you hit me and ran. You sounded like it upsets you that I'm dating younger people."

For the supervisor problem we would suggest proceeding in a similar manner. Get the person alone later and say something of the following nature: "You know, earlier tonight, Jack, when you said something about my playing and strumming the guitar? It bothered me that you said, 'You people have a lot of musical ability.' I don't even play the guitar. Maybe you thought you were joking, but, anyway, I felt like you were putting me down and I wanted to let you know how I feel."

There is no reason to continue our description of these two instances further because they could go in a number of ways. Remember, however, that if you are assertive in all of the components of assertiveness mentioned earlier in the book (eye contact, voice qualities, content, etc.), chances are the air between the two of you can be cleared.

The Non-Verbal, Non-Assertive Put-Down

In counseling married couples, the use of role-playing procedures often brings to light excellent examples of non-assertive, non-verbal put-downs. Typically they are not consciously used to irritate the other person, but occur automatically. Two instances will illustrate this category.

EXAMPLE: GENERAL PUT-DOWN

Her: "I feel that you should call me if you are going to be late from work. Half the time I don't know whether you'll be home for dinner or not, and several times I've eaten alone after preparing a meal for both of us." (She pauses for a response.)

Him: (Staring at her and not responding. He keeps staring until she becomes self-conscious and diverts her eyes or feels he didn't understand and needs more information. She says nothing about his staring behavior.)

In this situation, his staring and not responding soon enough acted in effect as a put-down of what his mate said. It served to confuse her and make her feel vulnerable. In the future she could say something like:

Her: "Your staring throws me off, could you respond a little quicker?" *or* "Are you staring because you need more information?"

EXAMPLE: MINORITY PUT-DOWN (CHILD)

A twelve-year-old's room is all messed up with clothes on the floor, an unmade bed, etc. His/her father comes into the room, looks at the mess, grimaces, shrugs his shoulders while turning his palms up, and turns to leave.

Son/Daughter: "Hey, Dad, it looks like something is bothering you."

Dad: "Yeah, it's this big mess. Why don't you clean it up?"

Son/Daughter: "Okay. I'm studying right now, but I'll get to it in a few minutes. Could I say something about what just happened between us, though?"

Dad: "Sure, what's wrong?"

Son/Daughter: "Well, I wish you would say what you're thinking when you come in, instead of looking upset and shrugging your shoulders. It's hard for me to know what you're thinking."

One of the most important methods in the above examples is seeking clarification from the other person if you suspect a put-down. Therefore, in the *robbing the cradle* situation you say, "What do you mean?" And in the *staring* situation you could ask, "Are you staring because you need more information?" There are two reasons to seek clarification. First, you may find out that you are misinterpreting someone's message as a put-down when in fact it is not meant as one. Second, by seeking clarification you can sometimes level or "straighten up" the other person. That is, if you catch them at their game of indulging in put-down behavior, even though it usually is not done purposefully, they have to shape up and treat you as an equal. In either case, if you say nothing, you give silent approval for them to put you down again, if that is what they are doing, the next time around.

The verification to avoid misinterpretation is extremely important because so often we assume something is meant by a response and then "go" on that belief system even though we may be wrong. Two instances will help show you what we mean.

One of our female clients went into a store to assert

herself about a bill, and during the interchange the saleswoman looked up her name on their records. When she found our client's name, she discovered that she had known her to some extent several years before. "Are you Jane Brown?" she asked. When our client said, "Yes, I am," the clerk said, "Well, you certainly don't look the same!" The conversation continued and as Jane was about to leave, the clerk repeated again, "Well, you certainly don't look the same!" Unfortunately Jane was confused and truly didn't know what the saleswoman meant by her statement, but she did not check it out. Instead she took it as a negative comment about her looks, inferring that she had changed for the worse. The key point, however, is that she didn't ask for clarification.

The second example comes from an interpersonal group setting. One person, Susan, was spending a good deal of time talking about feelings toward her parents. All during the discussion another person, Joe, sat across the room frowning and grimacing. After she had finished, the group started to shift to another topic.

The group leader then asked: "Susan, did you see how Joe was reacting to your talking?"

Susan: "Yes, you mean his silent language?"

Group Leader: "Mhm. How did you interpret it?"

Susan: "Oh, I'm sure he didn't like what I was saying; maybe he was bored."

Joe (laughing): "No, that's not it at all. I was just remembering how my own parents treated me in exactly the same ways. I was with you all the way."

This example from the non-verbal area points out again the necessity of checking out your interpretations. Don't assume, don't guess, just ask and find out. By assertively inquiring or trying to verify, we can learn the truth.

We hasten to point out that we are not trying to

eliminate all non-verbal communication. Some non-verbal messages help to liven up your verbal expression. We feel it is wise to begin watching your own non-verbal messages, however, to make sure that they are in fact enhancing your verbal messages. If the two are incongruent, not working together, be careful. Essentially the more you practice expressing your true feelings assertively, the less you have to put others down or cover up by passive non-verbal messages. Keep using the active, facilitating messages like a smile when you are happy, a frown when angry, raised eyebrows when puzzled, good hand gestures, and so on.

Now we'll discuss put-downs from yourself.

The Overt Put-Down

This simply means that when we are around other people we will verbally and oftentimes non-verbally give out messages that put ourselves down. As an example, Kathi is listening to Sharon describe how she performs in water skiing, basketball, and so on. At the end of the description Kathi says something like:

"Oh, Sharon, that is really great. I could never do anything like that; I can't even play Ping Pong."

Non-verbally, Kathi might hang her head or shrug her shoulders as she talks.

As you read the above example I'm sure you can remember hundreds of others that you use or have seen others use. It is almost automatic for most of us to use put-down behavior on ourselves. We put ourselves down for being clumsy, for being fat, for being dumb, for looking like a mess, etc. Many of us are so bad that we cannot even accept a compliment without overtly putting ourselves down. Listen to the following:

Jason has just won first prize in a photography contest. His friend Jerry comes up and says: "Hey, Jason,

I heard you won that contest. That's neat, there must have been a lot of competition. I'm proud of you."

Jason replies: "Oh no, there wasn't much to it. I think it was luck actually. I'm really an amateur." As Jason talks he may shake his head negatively, shuffle his feet, look down, blush and so on.

The Covert Put-Down

With this type of response we keep to ourselves the belief or feeling that we are no good, lousy, stupid, ugly, have no talent, can't do this or that, and so on. That inner tape recording starts off whenever we make a mistake, or compare ourselves with others, or are verbally put down by another, or fail at something we are trying to do, or think about all of our past "goof-ups" and so on. As in the area of covert put-downs, most of us are past masters of this downgrading type of behavior. Let's look at one example.

Terry has been working on putting together an engine he has been trying to fix. One part will not go in, no matter how hard he tries. In his mind, he hears this little voice say, "You are really dumb; you've put this together many times before. Come on, get on the ball. I'll bet Tommy would have had it done long ago, etc."

Nothing constructive can come out of putting yourself down either overtly or covertly. What good does it do? It doesn't make you a better person, does it? Quite the contrary: isn't your self-confidence hurt by downing yourself too much? Learn to listen to your inner and your outer language and start catching yourself when you slip into put-downs. Practice not engaging in self-put-down behavior. Try to be nicer to yourself. Like yourself. Spot those put-down phrases before they get too far into your mind or out of your mouth. Be assertive with yourself and think and say self-fulfilling thoughts instead of self-deprecating ones. There is a game Dr. Emmons' children are playing these days which goes like this: after someone says something silly, funny, or stupid: "Ha, ha, ha, you are what you say, you are what you say!" Perhaps there is more truth in that than we are willing to accept.

17

Very Personal Assertions—Caring and Joy

This is the hardest chapter to write. Somehow, neither as a society nor as individual human beings have we dealt very well with this most important topic of all. In the first edition of *Your Perfect Right,* we didn't even try to expand on the topic. "Stand up for yourself" was the slogan of assertive behavior therapy. There are those among our colleagues who still hold that positive caring expressions are outside the definition of "assertive" behavior. A faculty colleague of ours responded to a notice of our assertion training groups by asking if we were "teaching the students to talk back to their teachers." (We hope so, but so much more as well!)

In a review of that first edition of *Your Perfect Right,* written for the professional journal *Behavior Therapy,* Dr. Michael Serber commented upon our oversight. The late clinical director at Atascadero (California) State Hospital, psychiatrist Serber was himself a pioneer in developing assertive training, and a considerable influence on our work. He wrote:

> Certainly, behavioral skills necessary to stand up to the multiple personal, social, and business situations confronting the majority of people are imperative to master. But what of other just as necessary skills, such as being able to give and

take tenderness and affection? Is not the expression of affection toward other people also assertion? There are many behavior modifiers who are completely "turned off" to sensitivity-training groups. The majority of such groups, if they try to teach anything, do it in such a haphazard, discontinuous fashion that it is difficult to imagine anything concrete being learned. Nevertheless, the content of sensitivity training, the ability to express warmth and affection, to be able to give and take feelings, including anger, badly needs the special attention behavior modifiers can bring to it. Sensitivity training can become a unique area in which humanistic goals and behavioral techniques can yield both meaningful and concrete new behaviors.

We have found that expressing *positive, caring* feelings is often more difficult for non-assertive and aggressive persons (and for many otherwise assertive persons) than "standing up" behavior. Particularly for adults, positive expressions are often inhibited. Embarrassment, fear of rejection or ridicule, the "superiority of reason over emotion" are all excuses given to explain the inhibition of spontaneous expressions of warmth, caring, and love.

Freedom of positive expression has not been encouraged in our culture. As we discussed in Chapter 4, polite restraint is the accepted order of things. Nevertheless, the new lifestyles and youth subcultures, which have been most obvious among potent forces for change, encourage greater spontaneity. We heartily endorse greater openness in the communication of genuine positive feeling toward other persons.

The uninhibited freedom of movement which is encouraged by modern music and dance forms is another positive step toward allowing us to openly express happiness and joy. Young people, blacks, and Latinos all seem to be considerably freer in demonstrating warmth and positive emotions than are adult members of the majority white population.

The difficulty some persons have in saying "thank you" is at once amazing and very sad. Wayne, an acquaintance of ours who heads a multi-million-dollar giant organization, is noted for almost never expressing appreciation to the people who work for him. A job well done is seldom rewarded in any overt manner. Wayne is evidently afraid to act in a warm positive fashion—perhaps because he might appear "soft," or maybe because others might come to *expect* some sort of praise for their efforts. Needless to say, morale in the organization is not particularly high.

Why are we so afraid of caring? What makes it so difficult for me to say to you that I really enjoy your friendship? Why is reaching out to another person— even to say "hello"—such an onerous chore?

We seem to have a really mixed-up view of "love" in Western culture. It gets all tangled up with sex and becomes a source of embarrassment, fear, and taboo. If somehow another person's company is genuinely satisfying, enjoyable, or exciting, society suggests that we'd better look for something wrong, be careful, hold back. "Don't take a risk, you might get hurt."

Surely it is possible to genuinely care for—love— another person without "romantic" involvement! What a narrow view of love that allows only for romantic/sexual relationships! An important public official in California has been the object of scorn and ridicule for signing letters to other public officers with the closing "Love, . . ." How sad for us that we cannot tolerate the concept of love between persons outside of the romantic context. Erich Fromm has done a significant service for us all in his book *The Art of Loving,* in which he differentiates between five types of love: fraternal, maternal, erotic, love of God, and self-love. Perhaps we can begin to allow ourselves to "love one another" more freely if we see love in its broader context.

Let's begin at the beginning, however, with your positive feelings toward yourself. Can you give expression to the feeling of elation which accompanies the achievement of a highly valued personal goal? Do you allow yourself the pleasure of feeling satisfied with a job well done? Of making someone else happy? Of congratulating yourself? Remember Chapter 3 for a moment: "A Behavioral Model for Personal Growth." How are you treating yourself? Can you honestly answer those questions and say you are behaving in a caring, loving way toward *yourself?* We are increasingly convinced that a key element of assertive behavior is *being assertive with yourself!* Caring enough for yourself to *believe* you can, then *doing it.* In the therapeutic setting, we overcome a lack of self-love by *authorizing* the assertive behavior. As discussed in Chapter 8, the result of the "authorized" action is an enhanced concept of self-worth, which is the beginning of a positive turn in the attitude-behavior-feedback-attitude cycle. Encouragement from a professional therapist enables a person to begin acting more assertively. *You* can achieve the same results on your own or with a minimum of help by following the procedures we have described.

Say It Out Loud!

Expressing your positive feelings for another person is a highly assertive act. And, as with other assertions we have noted, the act itself—that is, *doing it*—is more important by far than the words you use or your

own style of communication. This is even more true
for expressions of caring. Nothing represents a more
personal, individual expression than that which says,
"You mean a great deal to me at this moment."

Consider some ways of communicating that message:

A warm, firm, and extended handshake. (Ever
notice the duration and feeling of a "brotherhood"
hand clasp—e.g., Black Power, fraternity members?)

A hug, the squeeze of an arm, an arm around the
shoulders, an affectionate pat on the back, the squeeze
of a hand held affectionately.

"Thank you."

"You're great!"

"I really understand what you mean."

A warm smile.

Extended eye contact.

"I'm here."

A gift of love (made by the giver, or uniquely special to the recipient, etc.).

"I believe you."

"I trust you." (Better yet, an *act* of trust.)

"I love you."

"I believe in you."

"I'm glad to see you."

"I've been thinking of you."

"You've been on my mind."

Probably none of these messages is a new thought
to you. Yet you may find it difficult to allow yourself
to say or do them. It is too easy to be hung up on
embarrassment, or to assume: "She knows how I feel,"
or "He doesn't care to hear that." But *who* doesn't
care to hear that? All of us need to know we are
cared about and admired and needed. If those around
us are *too* subtle in their expressions of positive regard,
we can too easily begin to doubt, and perhaps look

elsewhere for what the Transactional Analysis people call our "strokes"—positive feedback from others.

We recently asked a group of university students to identify for us some of the experiences which were rewarding for them—what made each of them feel especially good. Here are some of their favorite "strokes" (notice how many involve someone else expressing a caring thought!):

Praise
Payoff
Assurance
Encouragement
Independence
Security
Recognition
Appreciation
Affection
Friendliness
Achievement
Getting an A on an exam
Having someone say "hello"
Receiving a compliment
Giving a compliment
Having a friend
Helping others
Laughter
Spoken affirmation
Implementation of ideas
Request to repeat a job previously done

Making new friends
Positive comment
Touch
Satisfaction
Approval
Reward
Jobs completed
Recognition when speaking
Greeting someone else
Singing
Keeping my plants alive
Good grades
Compliments from the opposite sex
Personal satisfaction with myself
My boyfriend's/girl-friend's actions of love toward me
Expressed interest of others
Acceptance of an invitation

Despite the obvious importance to each of us of *hearing* positive feedback from others, we encounter in therapy so many people who are unhappy precisely because they lack such response from someone who cares.

In very intimate relationships, between lovers for example, it is often assumed that each partner "knows" the feelings of the other. Such assumptions often lead to the marriage counselor's office, with complaints such as, "I never know how he feels;" "She never tells me she loves me;" "We just don't communicate any more." Frequently it is necessary only to reestablish a communication pattern in which each partner is expressing *overtly* his/her feelings—particularly those of caring. The expression of caring is seldom a panacea for all the ills of an ailing marriage, but can shore up the foundation by helping each partner to remember what was good about the relationship in the first place!

Ellen and Doug are a good example—maybe we should say a *bad* example!—of a couple who built their relationship primarily upon assumptions. During the courtship and honeymoon days, of course, each wanted to make a good impression on the other. Their style was to say very little, or to be very positive and enthusiastic about *anything* suggested by the other. The result was a double façade—neither knew what the partner was *really* thinking or feeling.

Doug had been raised in a family where few emotions were displayed. Ellen, on the other hand, was fairly insecure and needed constant reassurance of Doug's caring for her. When he failed to tell her of his love—which was common, since he had never learned such expressiveness—she felt he did *not* love her. Doug, for his part, resented Ellen's demands for attention. Love can be a problem, even for those who are experiencing it!

Psychologists Herbert A. Otto and George R. Bach have developed extensive systems for improving spontaneous expression of caring in intimate relationships. Readers particularly interested in pursuing this area further are referred to their works, noted in the Suggested Reading section.

Good Show!

Compliments are a frequent source of discomfort for non-assertive and aggressive persons. To offer to someone else kind words about him/herself as a person or about something done for you may be a difficult thing for you. Again, we encourage *practice* of that which causes you some anxiety. Go out of your way to praise others—not dishonestly or insincerely, but whenever a genuine opportunity presents itself. Don't concern yourself with waiting for the "right words" either. Your thoughtfulness—the honest expression of what you are feeling—will convey itself with almost any vehicle *if you act!* Try simply, "I like what you did," or "Neat!" or a big smile.

Accepting compliments—to hear someone else direct a very positive statement to you, or about you to a third person—is perhaps an even more challenging task, particularly difficult if you are not feeling good about yourself. Nevertheless, it is an assertive act—a mutually enhancing response—to accept praise from another person.

Consider first that you really have no right to deny that person his/her perception of you. If you say, "Oh, you just caught me on a good day!" or "It wasn't anything special," or "It was an accident that it turned out well," you have, in effect, told the complimenter that she/he has poor judgment, that she/he *is wrong*. That person, too, has a right to feelings, and if he/she is positive toward you, do him/her—and yourself—the service of accepting.

We are not suggesting that you go about praising yourself, or accepting credit for achievements which are not your own. We do feel, however, that when another person sincerely wishes to convey a positive comment about you, you allow the expression of that feeling without rejection or qualification. Try saying at the least, "It's hard for me to accept that, but thank you;" or better yet is simply, "That feels good," or "I like to hear that."

If you can begin to give and receive genuine affection for other persons, if you can allow yourself to hear positive things about you, if you can share your own joy with another, and glow with one who is joyous, you will experience a quality of life which makes all other assertive acts pale by comparison.

And the paradox is, all you have to do to achieve *this* is to relax and let it happen!

Reaching Out

At a large gathering of people, you find no familiar faces. Suddenly a stranger comes up to you and begins a conversation, relieving your anxiety and "lost" feeling.

Two days after you move into a new neighborhood, the couple next door appear at your house with a loaf of freshly baked bread and a pot of coffee.

As you look in vain for a street sign in a foreign land, a native approaches you and says: "May I help you find your way?"

Such thoughtful acts can produce a warm feel ing for the person who was assertive enough to reach out. We often hesitate to initiate contact in these ways, for much of the same reason we fail to assert ourselves in other circumstances—we are afraid of being rejected. Perhaps, you may say to yourself, that stranger at the party is looking for someone in particular, and I would just get in the way. So you both remain alone.

The new neighbors, you and your spouse decide, would rather become acquainted "gradually"—"when we meet by accident while putting out the garbage cans." As a result of your hesitation, they see the community as distant and not very friendly.

And the foreign visitor returns home convinced that people in this country are indeed aloof and do not help travelers from other lands.

Taking the initiative in these and similar situations is a difficult assertive act, one that requires both a degree of concern for the other person and some courage of your own. Yet, when you reach a point at which you are able to be the initiator of conversation, the one who does reach out to others, you are at a high level of assertiveness.

We ask members of our assertive behavior groups to perform several acts requiring initiative. It is strange how at once easy and difficult it is to begin a conversation with a stranger. How easy, for example, to approach someone who is sitting on a bus, plane, or in a theater, and ask, "Is this seat vacant?" Yet you may not recognize that having asked the question *you have started a conversation!* The ice is broken, the barrier crossed, and one need merely keep the ball rolling at that point ("Where are you headed?" "Where is your home?" "How long have you been waiting?" "My name is John Doe/Mary Roe").

Yet we make these circumstances difficult by *assuming*. (She doesn't want to talk to me. I don't have anything to say. He'll tell me to go to hell. My voice will sound funny. An earthquake will swallow us both up if I dare speak.) Such assumptions are almost never valid, but they can be checked out merely by asking! Don't depend on reading the other person's mind. Find out for yourself by taking the risk and reaching out! It's another important way to care about yourself and others.

As we have discussed caring and reaching out to others in this chapter you may have seen these situations as no problem for you. Great! We hope you find that expressing positive regard for others is easy to do, and that you do so routinely and without difficulty.

If on the other hand you are one of those who are inhibited about showing that you care—either because you fear rejection or because you don't want to be seen as "soft"—we urge you to apply the principles of Chapter 7 to learning to express your positive feelings for others. Even if the response is not what you may hope for—you may find the giving to be its own reward.

III

Beyond Self-Assertion

God, give us the serenity to accept what cannot be changed, the courage to change what should be changed, and the wisdom to distinguish the one from the other.

—*Reinhold Niebuhr*

18 _____

Helping Others To Learn Assertion

As you have progressed through this book and as you have practiced assertion in your own life, you have probably become aware of assertion, non-assertion, and aggression in yourself and in others. In this chapter we are concerned with how you can help those around you to develop assertiveness as you yourself become more and more aware. If you buy a new hat or a different car, for instance, all of a sudden you find yourself becoming aware of how many people have a hat or a car just like yours. The same is true of learning a new skill like assertiveness. As you become familiar with good eye contact, proper use of voice, appropriate ways to speak your feelings and the other methods we have suggested, you will find yourself recognizing the good and bad approaches which others use in dealing with people.

We feel that it is natural to want to help others to learn a new skill. Remember back in your own life? Who taught you to ride a bike, to sew, to cook, to build, to read, to dance? Chances are it was a friend, a parent, a brother or sister, much of the time. So often our learning is not acquired from a qualified professional teacher; rather, it is a product of our own natural setting.

Typically, as with most of the above examples, the

skills we learn are not interpersonal skills. This, of course, is why our discussion here is so vital. The concepts of assertiveness are basic enough so that you can teach yourself and others. Assertion is a skill that can be learned just like any other skill. It does not make any difference that it concerns people-to-people skills rather than people-to-objects skills.

How often do you find yourself in situations where someone is complaining about something that happened between him and another person? At your weekly card group, do certain individuals gossip about the faults of their mate or about how Stan or Stella down the street did such and such a thing to them? Or do your co-workers gossip about each other's faults or complain about how the boss treats them? What if you are out with a friend and discover that he/she is non-assertive or aggressive in an actual situation? Perhaps you can readily see that every time Joe talks to his father he gets "dumped on" or that Jackie is quite frequently quick-tempered with her boyfriend.

Instead of continually listening to others complain or observing them operate at less than optimum, why not try to be helpful? Essentially the situation is already out in the open anyway; it is usually easy to see that the person is not approaching the situation in the best way. Why not offer assertive ways for that person to handle his/her own difficulties?

Suppose you are out shopping with your mother and the clerk gives her a hard time? What should you do if your mother is quick-tempered with the clerk or does the opposite and knuckles under? You may wish that your mother could only know how to be assertive. Why should you suffer in silence (being non-assertive) when perhaps you could say something later?

Helping the Non-Assertive Mom

Son or Daughter: "Say, Mom, remember earlier when that clerk gave you a hard time, and you didn't say anything?"

Mother: "Oh, that wasn't anything; it really didn't bother me much."

Son or Daughter: "Well, you know I used to think the same thing until I read a book about learning how to stand up for myself."

Mother: "Oh, I couldn't do that. I don't want to cause any trouble or hurt anyone."

Son or Daughter: "That's the great part about being assertive, Mom. You don't have to hurt anyone. Here, let me show you how I might have handled the clerk."

Helping the Aggressive Mom

Son or Daughter: "Hey, Mom, remember earlier when that clerk gave you a hard time and you got pretty upset?"

Mother: "Well, that idiot sure deserved it. Imagine treating me that way; and I've gone there for years, too!"

Son or Daughter: "Okay, you're right. But I felt like you hurt that person's feelings, and you could have done the same thing in a better way."

Mother: "Don't try to tell *me* what to do, youngster! I've been through a lot more than you have!"

Son or Daughter: "Now don't get mad. Just let me show you this one time how I might have done it."

From this point on, in either of the cases given above, you would proceed as the individual situation allows. Try to follow the basic principles in this book. Our step-by-step process is important but flexible, depending on the responses of the person we are teaching. In the case of your aggressive mom, for instance, you may not get beyond talking to her about the situation and suggesting that she read this book.

Let us now show you how we might handle a client with a particular problem so you can observe our step-by-step process in action.

One-to-One Facilitation

Step 1:   Identify the situation that needs attention. Example:

Client: "This one boy has called me twice to ask me out and he just won't take my hints. I don't want to hurt his feelings by telling him the truth; what should I do when he calls again?"

Step 2:   Set up the scene. Work with the client to structure closely the potential situation, in order to present the covert scene accurately and to simulate the feelings one has in the real situation. Example:

Facilitator: "You've decided you don't like him?"

Client: "No, he's a nice person, but we just don't have the same interests. Besides, I'm not attracted to him physically. I can't tell him that, though; it would crush him."

Step 3:   Present the situation to the person for covert rehearsal. Example:

Fa: "Are you sure? I'd like for you to go over the situation in your imagination now. Close your eyes and imagine yourself receiving the next call. Let yourself respond in whatever way you feel."

Cl: (Silent, imagines scene.)

Step 4: Model an assertive response for the particular situation. Present audio and video models if available. You may wish to tape your modeling here also. Example:

Fa: "Now I'll show you *one* way to approach him. Pretend I am you and you are him. Call me."

Fa: "Hello, this is Y."

Cl: "Hi, this is X . . . *(small talk)* . . . Say, there is a great movie playing downtown on Friday, and I would love to have you go with me. I'll be so disappointed if you can't go."

Fa: "I really am busy on Friday, but I've been wanting to talk to you about us anyway, X. I feel I have been misleading you, and I want to straighten things out. I really am concerned about hurting you, but I don't see any future in our relationship."

Cl: "Why? What have I done wrong?"

Fa: "That's just it; you've done nothing wrong. I feel that our interests aren't the same, and I'm not really attracted to you."

Cl: "Oh." (Pause.)

Fa: "I hope you aren't too disappointed, but I had to be honest with you, so I wouldn't hurt you more later."

Cl: "Well, I appreciate that anyway. So, I guess I shouldn't call you any more."

Fa: "That would be best."

Cl: "Good-bye."

Fa: "Bye."

Cl: "What if he hangs up halfway through the conversation?"

Fa: "If you are truly assertive, most likely that

won't occur; but if it does, that is just the way it has to be."

Step 5:   Answer the client's questions about how you handled the situation. Point out the differences between assertive versus non-assertive and aggressive responses. Stress non-verbal factors if they are pertinent. Discuss client's ethical or philosophical concerns. Example:

Cl: "Wouldn't it be better to tell white lies like 'I have to wash my hair' so he'll get the hint?"

Fa: "You've tried hints already and they haven't worked. Even if they eventually did work, you actually are hurting him and yourself more in the long run by not being honest with your feelings."

Step 6:   Repeat Step 3. Covert rehearsal based on the client's use of an effective model for handling the situation. Encourage client to imagine a positive outcome.

Step 7:   Rehearse the scene once again. This time the client role-plays him/herself. Audio or video tape if possible.

Step 8:   Go over the performance. Provide feedback and coaching where needed. Don't forget positive reinforcement. Example:

Fa: "You did an excellent job. I liked the way you stuck to your point when he tried to persuade you to let him call again. Your voice was a little soft and somewhat shaky. Let's do it again and try to use a stronger voice."

Step 9:   Repeat Steps 4 through 8 as often as needed. Alternate between modeling and role-playing and provide coaching so as to shape the behavior to a suitable point.

Step 10: The person is now ready to test the new response pattern in the actual situation. Up to this point the preparation has taken place in a relatively secure environment. Nevertheless, careful training and repeated practice have developed an almost automatic reaction to the situation. The client should thus be reassured if necessary and encouraged to proceed in the real-life situation. If he/she is unwilling to do so, further rehearsals may be needed. Example:

Fa: "How do you feel about using your new approach with him when he calls again?"

Cl: "I think I'm ready, and I know he's going to call."

Fa: "Well, I feel good about how you've handled it here, so I also think you're ready."

Step 11: The client should be encouraged to return as soon as practical following the real-life trial in order to review the effort. The therapist should reward whatever degree of success the person experiences, and offer continued assistance. Example:

Fa: "I want you to keep a record of how it goes, what he says, what you say, your feelings and so on. Then come in as soon as you can after it is over, so we can review how you did. Okay?"

Cl: "Okay."

Initially, then, the individual should begin with small assertions that are likely to be successful and rewarded, and from there proceed to more difficult assertions. Ideally each step should be explored with the facilitator until the client-trainee is capable of being fully in control of most situations. He should be warned against taking it upon his own initiative to attempt a difficult assertion at first without special preparation. The facilitator also should particularly beware of instigating an assertion where the trainee is likely to fail miserably, thus inhibiting further attempts at assertiveness.

If the trainee does suffer a setback, which very well may happen, the facilitator must be ready to help him to analyze the situation and regain his confidence. Especially in the early stages of assertion, trainees are prone to mistakes either of inadequate technique or of overzealousness to the point of aggression. Either miscue could cause negative results, particularly if the other individual, the "acted upon," becomes hostile and highly aggressive. Therefore, the facilitator must be prepared to serve as a buffer and to help reestablish motivation.

Most trainees will have more than one specific problem with being assertive. In the above case, for example, the girl may have difficulty returning items to a store, gaining her rights with roommates, etc. The same basic process with variations may be used for each situation. The individuality of the client must always be accommodated. Facilitators are encouraged to provide a learning environment in which the trainee may grow in assertiveness, and carefully to avoid "shoving it down his throat."

Obviously you will not be able to go through all of the steps given above. The most important steps are (1) modeling a way to deal with the situation, (2) having the person role-play how they would handle it, and (3) offering constructive feedback or suggestions about how the person performed.

When helping another person to be assertive, observe the following hints on what not to do as you proceed.

When Helping Others To Be Assertive . . .

(1) *Don't force the person to try assertiveness.*
Approach others and offer your help assertively, but
back off if they don't want your help. No matter how
obvious it is that they could use assertiveness, it is
their life.

(2) *Don't place judgments on the person.* Avoid
telling them that what they are doing is silly or stupid
or foolish or cowardly or chicken. Simply ask if you
can show them another way to approach the problem.

(3) *Don't play the role of Junior Therapist.* Don't
get in over your head. Try to encourage the generally
non-assertive or the generally aggressive person to go
for professional help. Don't interpret his/her behavior
or symptoms. Don't attempt to psychoanalyze anyone.

(4) *Don't try to cover too much ground at one
time.* Keep the situation as well-defined and simple as
possible. Don't let someone dominate your time; set
your limits. Work on only one situation at a time.
Don't try to work on all of someone's assertive problems at once.

19

Forming an Assertive Group

The main method we use to teach assertion in our work is through conducting assertive training groups. The process of assertive behavior development may be very effectively applied in a group setting. With many people this approach is more effective than one-to-one training because of the expanded potential for interaction with others during the training program.

As you have read about assertion, you may have thought: "I'll bet my youth group could spend some time talking about and practicing assertion," or "Maybe our whole family should get together regularly for several weeks and try out being assertive with each other." The opportunities are endless. Almost any functioning group—be it a church group, a consciousness-raising group, a Scouting group, an encounter group, a spiritual awareness group—can benefit from learning about and practicing assertion together. On the other hand, perhaps you can form your own assertive group from people you know who want to increase their ability to deal with others and feel more self-confident. There might be several of your roommates or friends or co-workers who would like to get together for an assertive group.

Several specific advantages result from a small group. The non-assertive or aggressive person, as we have already demonstrated, typically encounters great anxiety in certain life situations when he is faced with confronting other people in order to assert himself. Learning assertiveness in a group provides a laboratory of other people with whom to work. By discovering that they share similar problems, each is less alone. A group is typically understanding and supportive—a social environment in which each person can be accepted as he is, and thus be comfortable enough to experiment with new behavior.

With several individuals undertaking assertive training together, there is a broader base for social modeling. Each person sees several others learning to act assertively, and each is able to learn from the strengths and weaknesses of the others.

A group provides greater opportunities for feedback than can an individual person who is trying to help. Hearing reactions from several different people can speed the learning process for each member.

Social situations involving a number of people are a frequent source of anxiety for both aggressive and non-assertive persons. Work in a group provides a realistic opportunity to face several people and overcome that difficulty in a relatively safe training environment.

The group is, of course, a powerful source of social reinforcement for each of its members. Knowing several others are "expecting" his/her growth and active effort toward assertiveness, each member is stimulated to greater achievement than if he were solely "on his own." And, for its part, the group rewards new assertiveness with all the force of its social approval.

Now listen to how we proceed when we conduct assertive groups in our work as counseling psychol-

ogists. As you read, try to see how you might adapt
the format to fit your own particular group.

The Make-up of Assertive Training Groups

Our typical assertive training group has from five to
twelve members. Fewer than five restricts the potential for social modeling, limits the sources of feedback,
and fails to provide the range of behavior style needed
for each client to experience a variety of others as
he/she tries out new assertive behaviors. We prefer,
when possible, to balance the number of men and
women in our groups, since social relationships with
the opposite sex are a frequent source of anxiety for
our non-assertive and aggressive clients. A group with
equal numbers of each sex enhances opportunity for
helping its members to deal effectively with social
situations involving the opposite sex.

Because we function in a university counseling center, our groups are usually scheduled to coincide with
the academic term. Thus we typically meet one hour
twice each week for eight or nine weeks—a total of
sixteen to eighteen hours. Recently we have experi-
mented with two alternatives to this approach. We
have conducted a group for five or six weeks (10 or
12 one-hour sessions), then suspended meetings for
approximately three weeks, getting together again toward the end of the term for a follow-up meeting.
This approach appears to be as successful as our
longer-term groups. The basic concepts of assertion
can easily be covered and practiced within this short
period of time. Motivation tends to remain high for
both the leader and members; absenteeism is almost
non-existent. The break allows members time to identify any major obstacles which may need more attention. If necessary, further work with assertion on a

one-to-one basis can be arranged. In selected cases
additional therapeutic measures may also be needed.
We have also worked on a two-hour-once-a-week
schedule. The latter has the advantage of a longer and
often more intensive session, but the longer interval
between sessions seems to be a significant loss to the
behavior shaping process. Ideally, perhaps one-and-
one-half hours twice each week would best achieve
the goals of an assertive behavior group (we have no
controlled experimental data to support this conclusion, however).

Groups led by coleaders are, in our experience,
more effective environments for client growth than
those led by individual leaders. The dropout rate is
lower, enthusiasm higher, and both self-report and
leader observation of growth are greater. We have
worked with each other, with other staff counselors,
and with M.A.-level counselor-trainees. Coleaders are
most effective when they are open and honest with
each other and with group members, possess com-
plementary skills and facilitation styles, and are both
openly enthusiastic about assertive training. In addition, although we have been consistently most effective
in assertive groups when working together, we encourage a male-female coleader team. Effective models of
assertiveness of each sex are valuable resources for
assertive behavior groups.

The Assertive Training Process in Groups

The first session of our assertive training groups is
devoted to a lecture presentation on assertive behavior,
followed by the usual round of introductions of group
members.

Opening with background material on what the
group will be all about, we utilize the non-assertive-

aggressive-assertive description given in Chapters 2 and 4. We call attention to the behavior-attitude cycle in Chapter 4, and point out the importance of practice with support and reinforcement from the group. Members are cautioned that assertive training is not a panacea, and that they will not discover miraculous changes overnight. They are also told that occasional failure is to be expected, but will not stop long-term progress.

We give several typical examples to illustrate our contention that assertiveness is a better way than the other two alternatives. Next, we indicate how the group will be structured, outlining the exercises in which each will participate. We request that members keep an ongoing log of their progress emphasizing specific, detailed examples. In summing up, we give a basic pep talk about becoming thoroughly involved in changing, the need for risk-taking, and the progress others have made. Throughout, we encourage the participants to ask questions, even though getting a group of primarily non-assertive people to initiate questions is often difficult. At this time, each member is asked to write down specific behaviors within our non-assertive-aggressive-assertive framework which they wish to change.

Upon the completion of these preliminaries one of us (the more assertive) states that it is time to go around the group and introduce ourselves. Even this initial exercise is handled as a demonstration of the learning process to be used in the group. The leader asks members to close their eyes and visualize themselves completing the task at hand. When all have finished, she/he then models the self-introduction, emphasizing personal background and reasons for being involved in an assertive group. The covert step is then repeated, after which we go around with the self-introduction, including the co-therapist. Finally, we discuss what has taken place, giving impressions about how the exercise proceeded, and pointing out that this will be the style of operation for this group (covert, modeling, role-playing).

The format established in the first group meeting with the introductions exercise is followed throughout the life of the assertive training group: a situation is posed; the members are asked to fantasize their individual responses to it; a model (often but not always the leader) role-plays the scene; the group briefly discusses the modeling behavior; a new covert response is called for; individual members role-play and are given feedback. Thus the three major facilitative components of assertive training (covert rehearsal, modeling, and role-playing or behavior rehearsal) are built in to the group learning process for each separate situation covered.

Following this pattern, the first few weeks of group meetings are structured so that each member participates in several fundamental exercises:

(1) Breaking into a small group of strangers already engaged in conversation at a party.

(2) Starting a conversation with a stranger in a classroom, on a bus, at a meeting. Maintaining a conversation.

(3) Returning faulty or defective items to a store.

(4) Being assertive with significant others: parents, roommates, spouses, boy/girlfriends.

(5) Asking someone to turn down a stereo that is too loud, or not talk so loudly in the library, theater, etc.

(6) Asking for a date/refusing a date on the telephone and face-to-face.

(7) Expressing positive feelings; "soft assertions."

(8) Speaking publicly.

(9) Learning how to argue with or stand up for oneself with a dominant or dogmatic and opinionated person.

We operate with considerable flexibility, and may leave out some situations or add others, according to the apparent needs of a particular group.

After each member of the group has completed the basic exercises, we encourage them to bring to the group current life situations which are troubling them. Although no one is denied the opportunity to present a personal situation earlier in the group process, we find that most participants, as in more traditional forms of group therapy, are reluctant to expose much of themselves very early in the life of the group. Thus it is usually more valuable to structure the first meeting, leaning more toward member-initiated activities after the learning process is well established and participants have come to trust one another more fully. At this point individual situations presented in the group frequently relate to intimate relationships:

How can I tell my father to stop nagging me?

How can I tell my boyfriend that I don't really love him?

My roommate has terrible B.O.!

My boss keeps making passes at me.

I yell at my wife and children every day when I get home from work.

No one pays any attention to me.

Such situations strike very close to home, of course, and are more sensitive and difficult to handle than the "clerk-in-the-store" variety, since they involve ongoing relationships with a great emotional investment. Sensitivity, patience, and careful attention to the principles of assertiveness—and to the consider-

ation of consequences—are in order here, and the
group leader is cautioned against pat solutions to
unique, individual problems. Under these conditions
other members of a perceptive and caring group are
often the most valuable resource to the therapist. In
any event, rehearsing approaches to significant others
is usually very worthwhile in the group, if only to gain
a better understanding of one's own feelings about the
person or situation. It is a rare group which does not
offer support and caring in delicate situations.

Practice in the expression of caring for another
(Chapter 17) is, of course, an important goal of assertive training. We focus considerable attention upon
the verbal expression of positive feelings toward oneself and others.

Similarly, at another point in the emotional spec-
trum, putting angry feelings into words is a useful
group exercise. We have encouraged group members
to practice anger (Chapter 12).

As our assertive behavior group nears the end of
its schedule, we assist each member to sensitize him/
herself to sources of continuing reinforcement for
assertion in his/her unique individual life environment. The group has been an important center of
support for the developing assertiveness of each member. Now, however, each must take responsibility for
identifying and expanding sources of support within
his/her own environment.

The final meeting of our assertive behavior training
group is usually devoted to a very positive uplifting
emotional experience developed by psychologist Herbert Otto: the "Strength Bombardment." Each member of the group is given approximately one minute to
speak about him/herself in only *positive* terms—no
qualifiers, no criticisms, no "buts." Immediately thereafter, the rest of the group gives to this member an

additional two minutes of *positive* feedback. The time may be varied to suit the group, but caution is urged: don't allow enough for embarrassing—and painful—silence. The clockwatcher can be flexible, but the important note is that this must be a positive experience for *each* member. The group leader needs to be prepared to fill any gaps in the feedback portion for the most "unlovable" group member, and to encourage the too-modest reluctant starter. The group leader is encouraged to be the first speaker in this exercise, as a model of self-assertion and to demonstrate appropriate positive statements to make about oneself.

Now that you have analyzed our format for conducting groups you are perhaps ready to look into the following points for your personal group. Each group is unique, but all should consider these factors.

Important Considerations When Starting Your Group

(1) *Selection of leaders.* As we stated above, coleaders seem to work best in our groups and preferably should be male-female. We feel that the leadership should be shifted to new coleaders at an appropriate time in order that all group members eventually have a chance to lead. Leadership is itself an act of assertion.

(2) *Establishing ground rules.* This is a point of vital concern. Group members should discuss and reach agreement on such things as the following:

How many meetings is a person allowed to miss before they are not allowed to return?

When should the group be closed to new members? After the first or second meeting? Or should membership always be kept open?

How long should individual meetings be and how often should you meet? Also, what will be the total overall time you will meet—five weeks, ten weeks, or what?

Will all information that group members decide to share be held as confidential? This is just as important in an assertive group as in any other group, and should be discussed.

Should the group members be required to have read this book, or can they attend now and read later? Will other reading be required?

(3) *Deciding on format.* We have given what we have found to be a successful way to conduct an assertive group. Our groups are highly structured; we follow our step-by-step process quite closely. Also, we practice the assertive situations given in this book, especially for the first four or five weeks of a group. Your group may decide differently, but all need to help make the decision. Other questions might center on having each keep a diary or log, having homework or not, and so on.

At this point it is important to review the list of Don't's given on page   which refer to helping one other person with assertion. They apply equally well to our work in groups.

In conclusion, keep in mind that you are forming an assertive group in order to work at making your lives better. Be careful that the group remains an assertive group where a good deal of practice takes place. Talking and discussing are fine, but they should not dominate the time. If you will work hard at improving yourself and others, the time you spend in the group will be among the warmest, most personally rewarding moments of your life.

Beyond Assertiveness

Our theme throughout this book has been the value of assertive behavior to the individual seeking self-direction in his life, and particularly in his interpersonal relationships. The perceptive reader will have recognized some of the potential shortcomings and hazards inherent in personal assertiveness. Sensitivity is required in taking into account some of these limitations and potentially negative consequences of asserting yourself.

Although assertive behavior will be its own reward for most, the consequences on occasion may deflate its value. Consider, for example, the young boy who assertively refuses the big bully's request to ride his new bike, and as a result finds himself nursing a black eye! His assertion was perfectly legitimate, but the other person was unwilling to accept the denial of *his* desire. Therefore, without suggesting that assertiveness be avoided if it appears hazardous, we do encourage persons to consider the probable consequences of their assertive acts. Under certain circumstances, the personal value of an assertion will be outweighed by the value of avoiding the probable response to that assertion.

It may be useful to review a number of possible situations in which the potential value of assertiveness is weighed against the likely consequences. It is our conviction that each person should be able to choose for himself how he will act. If an individual *can* act assertively under given conditions, but *chooses* not to, our purpose is accomplished. If he is *unable* to act assertively (i.e., cannot choose for himself how he will behave, but is cowed in non-assertiveness or triggered into aggressiveness), his life will be governed by others and his mental health will suffer.

Potential Adverse Reactions

In our experience with facilitating assertiveness in others we have found that negative results occur in very few instances. However, certain people do react in a disagreeable manner when they face assertion from another. Therefore, even if the assertion is handled properly, neither being non-assertive or aggressive, one may at times still be faced with uncomfortable situations such as the following:

(1) *Backbiting.* After you have asserted yourself, the other person involved may be somewhat disgruntled, but not openly. For example, if you see the others in line jumping ahead of you and you assert yourself, the person may grumble as he passes you to go to the end of the line. You may hear such things as "Who does he think he is anyway?" "Big deal!" "Big man!" "Queen bee!" and so forth. To our way of thinking, the best solution is simply to ignore the childish behavior. If you do retort in some manner, you are likely only to complicate the situation by reinforcing the fact that his/her words "got to you."

(2) *Aggression.* In this case the other party may become outwardly hostile toward you. Yelling or screaming could be involved, or physical reactions like bumping, shoving, or hitting. Again, the best approach

is to avoid escalating the condition. You may choose to express regret that he/she is upset by your actions, but you must remain steadfast in your assertion. This is especially true if you will have further contacts with the person. If you back down on your assertion, you will simply reinforce the negative reaction. As a result, the next time you assert yourself, the probability will be high that you will receive another aggressive reaction from the same person.

(3) *Temper tantrums.* In certain situations you may assert yourself with someone who has had his/her own way for a long period of time. He/she may then react to your assertion by looking hurt, saying his/her health is precarious, saying you don't like him/her, crying and feeling self-pity or otherwise attempting to control you by making you feel guilty.

(4) *Psychosomatic reactions.* Actual physical illness may occur in some individuals if you thwart a long-established habit. Abdominal pains, headaches, and feeling faint are just a few of the symptoms possible. To reiterate, however, one should choose to be firm in the assertion, recognizing that the other person will adjust to the new situation in a short time. You should also be consistent in your assertion whenever the same situation recurs with this individual. If you are inconsistent in asserting your rights, the other person involved will become confused. He or she may eventually just ignore your assertions.

(5) *Overapologizing.* On rare occasions, after you have asserted yourself, the other party involved will be overly apologetic or overly humble to you. You should point out that such behavior is unnecessary. If, in later encounters, he/she seems to be afraid of you or

overly deferential toward you, you should not take advantage of him/her. We feel that you could help the person to develop assertiveness, utilizing the methods we have described.

(6) *Revenge.* If you have a continuing relationship with the person to whom you have asserted yourself, there is the chance that he/she may seek revenge. At first it might be difficult to understand what he/she is attempting to do, but as time goes on, his/her taunts will become quite evident. Once you are certain that he/she is trying to make your life miserable, you should squelch his/her actions immediately. A recommended method is to take him/her aside and confront him/her directly with the situation. Usually this is enough to get him/her to cease his/her vengeful tactics.

Choosing Not To Assert Yourself

Choice is the key word in the assertion process. As long as you know in your own mind (from previous successful assertive encounters) that you *can* assert yourself, you may in a given instance decide not to do so. Following are some circumstances where one may choose non-assertiveness:

(1) *Overly sensitive individuals.* On occasion, from your own observations, you may conclude that a certain person is unable to accept even the slightest assertion. When this is apparent, it is much better to resign yourself to this fact than to chance an assertion. Although there are oversensitive types who use their apparent weakness to manipulate others, we are all aware that there are also certain individuals who are so easily threatened that the slightest disagreement causes them to explode, either inwardly (thus hurting

themselves) or outwardly (thus hurting others). You could avoid contact with such a person as much as possible, but if you must be around someone of this type, you may wish to accept him/her as he/she is and cause no friction, if such is feasible.

(2) *Redundancy*. Once in a while the person who has taken advantage of your rights will notice, before you get a chance to assert yourself, that he/she has done so. He/she will then remedy the situation in an appropriate way. Obviously, you should not wait for an extended period of time wishing that the other person will notice. Also, you should not hesitate to be assertive if he/she fails to make the amends which you feel should reasonably be made. If, on the other hand, you see that the person recognizes what has happened, it is not appropriate on your part to *then* pipe up and assert yourself.

(3) *Being understanding*. Now and then you may choose not to be assertive because you notice that the person is having difficulty; there can be extenuating circumstances. At a restaurant one evening, having ordered our meal a certain way, we noticed that the new cook was having great difficulty with everything. Therefore when our meal arrived, not exactly as we had ordered, we chose not to be assertive, rather than hassle him further. Another example is when someone you know is having an off day and is in a rare bad mood. In these cases you may *choose* to overlook things that may be going wrong between you, or postpone a confrontation to a more productive time. (Caution: It is easy to use "not wanting to hurt the other fellow's feelings" as a rationalization for non-assertiveness when assertion would be more appropriate. If you

find yourself doing this more than occasionally, we suggest that you carefully examine your real motives.)

When You Are Wrong

Especially in your early assertions, you may assert yourself when you have incorrectly interpreted a situation. Also, you may assert yourself with poor technique and offend the other person. If either of these situations does occur, you should be very willing to say that you have been wrong. There is no need to get carried away in making amends, of course, but you should be open enough to indicate that you know you have been mistaken. Additionally, you should not be apprehensive about future assertions with that person if you again feel that a situation calls for it.

Some Random Thoughts on Assertive Behavior

We have undertaken this book with continuing awareness of the moral and ethical ramifications of assertive behavior. The following comments are offered solely for consideration of these matters, to stimulate the reader's own thinking. The issues are complex and we make no pretense of having arrived at definitive answers even for ourselves.

Tolstoy has been credited with the observation that moral acts are distinguished from all other acts by the fact that they operate independently of any predictable advantage to ourselves or to others. This view can be applied to our thinking about assertive acts. The crucial question is: "Are there times in the life of every person when basic values must be sacrificed?"

Consider, for example, the following situation: You have undertaken a program that requires a long period of difficult work in preparation for a career or profession. This could be a trade apprenticeship; vocational schooling; night classes; studies in nursing, dentistry, medicine, law; or any other preparation for a career involving substantial investment of your time, energy and resources. Such a program has required not only time and effort, but it has used up most of your savings and caused you to become indebted in the process. Let us assume also that you are responsible for other persons, your children or dependents.

Near the end of your final year the vital qualifying test arrives, and you must demonstrate your knowledge, skills, and abilities. As you go through the testing procedure, you are doing very well until the end. Then a supervisor or examiner poses a question concerning an area of the program which is presently quite controversial. You know that this person is rigidly "set" in the belief that only one approach to the question is satisfactory and dislikes any challenge to this view. You have heard that several people have been flunked for holding opposite views. But you strongly believe a contrary view, and you are convinced that it will soon replace the older viewpoint.

Question: Should you compromise your values and answer the way the examiner wishes to hear, or should you severely jeopardize your future by standing up for your beliefs, even if it means risking failure and defeat?

If one considers it legitimate and necessary to compromise one's values in transitory instances, should one compromise over major issues that have long-term effects? Occasional lapses are to be expected, in our opinion, but to sacrifice one's views to those of others over a long time span is not in one's own ultimate best interest, nor is it moral.

Other persons must also be taken into consideration. What about one's dependents? If my assertion presents a serious hazard to the welfare of others for whom I am responsible, do I still have a right to assert my beliefs?

Are there positive immoral acts as well as negative ones? I know certain information about a subject being discussed in an English class that no one else knows or questions. Am I "morally non-assertive" if I decide not to seem "know-it-allish" and therefore say nothing of my special knowledge? Does the situation change if the class is in history? Psychology? Driver training? First aid? Pharmacology? Heart surgery?

Perhaps the key issue is whether or not the assertion, which one feels morally obligated to make, in actuality will make any difference. It might be better for all to accept the fact that some things are better left as they are. The quote introducing this section bears repeating here, for theologian Reinhold Niebuhr said it perhaps best of all: "God, give us the serenity to accept what cannot be changed, the courage to change what should be changed, and the wisdom to distinguish the one from the other."

Perhaps, in the final analysis, all I can change is myself. Yet if I *can* change myself into a more effectively assertive and emotionally honest person, that may prove to be the key to achievement of most of my goals in life.

Putting It All Together

It is hard to end this book. Again and again there seems to be "just one more thing" to say. One can never "say it all." Ultimately, the decision and the action come back to you, the reader. These pages only have meaning if they move you to bring about change in your own life.

Thousands have found in our suggestions a straightforward and effective system of growth toward greater personal assertiveness. Be encouraged; believe in your-self. When in doubt, remember the following sugges-tions. Review them from time to time. Then press on!

• Begin your own development of greater assertive-ness with small, achievable steps. You will start slowly, but your foundation will be solid and long-lasting, and you'll have greater long-range success.

• Being assertive doesn't always work (nothing *always* works!), but don't let setbacks stop you from trying. You will fail sometimes (so do we), but return again and again, starting with those small important steps.

• Remember to pat yourself on the back when you succeed in achieving even the smallest goal—and re-member that you *do* deserve to take the credit when you're the one who makes something happen!

• Ask for help when you need it. All of us need help at times, and it pays to get the best available. When in need, see a qualified professional counselor, clinical social worker, psychologist, or psychiatrist, and ask assertively about what help you can expect!

• Because there are as many examples as there are people, we have frequently had to generalize in this book. You are an individual, and what we have said in general may not apply directly to you. Cultural and ethnic backgrounds make a difference in what is con-sidered assertive. Sex, lifestyle, education, and occupa-tion are all relevant. Whatever the differences, you have a *choice* and you can be "in charge" in your own life. Assertive training cannot be all things to all people—it is one tool for helping people to become the persons they want to be, just as assertive behavior is one mode of expressing yourself.

• Keep in mind that any significant change comes slowly, with repeated practice. Be patient with yourself. Give yourself a chance!

• Assertiveness is more than standing up for yourself, or expressing your anger, or expressing your affection, or practicing scripts of what to say or do in given situations—it is your pattern of behavior and your feeling about yourself.

Ready now? Stand up! Speak out! Talk back! You'll like yourself better for it.

Suggested Reading

Alberti, R. E. and Emmons, M. L. *Your Perfect Right: A Guide to Assertive Behavior*. San Luis Obispo: Impact, 1970, 1974.

Bach, G. and Wyden, P. *The Intimate Enemy: How to Fight Fair in Love and Marriage*. New York: William Morrow & Co., Inc., 1968.

Fensterheim, H. *Help Without Psychoanalysis*. New York: Stein and Day, 1971.

Moriarty, T. "A Nation of Willing Victims," in *Psychology Today*, April, 1975.

Otto, H. *More Joy in Your Marriage*. New York: Hawthorn Books, Inc., 1969.

Phelps, S. and Austin, N. *The Assertive Woman*. San Luis Obispo: Impact, 1975.

Rogers, C. R. *On Becoming a Person*. New York: Houghton Mifflin Co., Inc., 1961.

Salter, A. *Conditioned Reflex Therapy*. New York: Farrar, Straus, 1949.

Wolpe, J. *The Practice of Behavior Therapy*. New York: Pergamon Press, 1969.

Appendix

THE UNIVERSAL DECLARATION
OF HUMAN RIGHTS

WHEREAS recognition of the inherent dignity and of the equal and inalienable rights of all members of the human family is the foundation of freedom, justice and peace in the world,

WHEREAS disregard and contempt for human rights have resulted in barbarous acts which have outraged the conscience of mankind, and the advent of a world in which human beings shall enjoy freedom of speech and belief and freedom from fear and want has been proclaimed as the highest aspiration of the common people,

WHEREAS it is essential, if man is not to be compelled to have recourse, as a last resort, to rebellion against tyranny and oppression, that human rights should be protected by the rule of law,

WHEREAS it is essential to promote the development of friendly relations between nations,

WHEREAS the peoples of the United Nations have in their Charter reaffirmed their faith in fundamental human rights, in the dignity and worth of the human person and in the equal rights of men and women and have determined to promote social progress and better standards of life in larger freedom,

WHEREAS Member States have pledged themselves to achieve, in cooperation with the United Nations, the promotion of universal respect for and observance of human rights and fundamental freedoms,

WHEREAS a common understanding of these rights and freedoms is of the greatest importance for the full realization of this pledge,

NOW, THEREFORE, THE GENERAL ASSEMBLY PROCLAIMS this Universal Declaration of Human Rights as a common standard of achievement for all peoples and all nations, to the end that every individual and every organ of society, keeping this Declaration constantly in mind, shall strive by teaching and education to promote respect for these rights and freedoms and by progressive measures, national and international, to secure their universal and effective recognition and observance, both among the peoples of Member States themselves and among the peoples of territories under their jurisdiction.

Article 1.   All human beings are born free and equal in dignity and rights. They are endowed with reason and conscience and should act towards one another in a spirit of brotherhood.

Article 2.   Everyone is entitled to all the rights and freedoms set forth in this Declaration, without distinction of any kind, such as race, colour, sex, language, religion, political or other opinion, national or social origin, property, birth or other status.

Furthermore, no distinction shall be made on the basis of the political, jurisdictional or international status of the country or territory to which a person belongs, whether it be independent, trust, non-self-governing or under any other limitation of sovereignty.

Article 3.   Everyone has the right to life, liberty and security of person.

Article 4.   No one shall be held in slavery or servitude; slavery and the slave trade shall be prohibited in all their forms.

Article 5.   No one shall be subjected to torture or to cruel, inhuman or degrading treatment or punishment.

Article 6.   Everyone has the right to recognition everywhere as a person before the law.

Article 7.   All are equal before the law and are entitled without any discrimination to equal protection of the law. All are entitled to equal protection against any discrimination in violation of this Declaration and against any incitement to such discrimination.

Article 8.   Everyone has the right to an effective remedy by the competent national tribunals for acts violating the fundamental rights granted him by the constitution or by law.

Article 9. No one shall be subjected to arbitrary arrest, detention or exile.

Article 10. Everyone is entitled in full equality to a fair and public hearing by an independent and impartial tribunal, in the determination of his rights and obligations and of any criminal charge against him.

Article 11. (1) Everyone charged with a penal offence has the right to be presumed innocent until proved guilty according to law in a public trial at which he has had all the guarantees necessary for his defence.

(2) No one shall be held guilty of any penal offence on account of any act or omission which did not constitute a penal offence, under national or international law, at the time when it was committed. Nor shall a heavier penalty be imposed than the one that was applicable at the time the penal offence was committed.

Article 12. No one shall be subjected to arbitrary interference with his privacy, family, home or correspondence, nor to attacks upon his honour and reputation. Everyone has the right to the protection of the law against such interference or attacks.

Article 13. (1) Everyone has the right to freedom of movement and residence within the borders of each state.

(2) Everyone has the right to leave any country, including his own, and to return to his country.

Article 14. (1) Everyone has the right to seek and to enjoy in other countries asylum from persecution.

(2) This right may not be invoked in the case of prosecutions genuinely arising from non-political crimes or from acts contrary to the purposes and principles of the United Nations.

Article 15. (1) Everyone has the right to a nationality.

(2) No one shall be arbitrarily deprived of his nationality nor denied the right to change his nationality.

Article 16. (1) Men and women of full age, without any limitation due to race, nationality or religion, have the right to marry and to found a family. They are entitled to equal rights as to marriage, during marriage and at its dissolution.

(2) Marriage shall be entered into only with the free and full consent of the intending spouses.

(3) The family is the natural and fundamental group unit

of society and is entitled to protection by society and the State.

Article 17. (1) Everyone has the right to own property alone as well as in association with others.

(2) No one shall be arbitrarily deprived of his property.

Article 18. Everyone has the right to freedom of thought, conscience and religion; this right includes freedom to change his religion or belief, and freedom, either alone or in community with others and in public or private, to manifest his religion or belief in teaching, practice, worship and observance.

Article 19. Everyone has the right to freedom of opinion and expression; this right includes freedom to hold opinions without interference and to seek, receive and impart information and ideas through any media and regardless of frontiers.

Article 20. (1) Everyone has the right to freedom of peaceful assembly and association.

(2) No one may be compelled to belong to an association.

Article 21. (1) Everyone has the right to take part in the government of his country, directly or through freely chosen representatives.

(2) Everyone has the right of equal access to public service in his country.

(3) The will of the people shall be the basis of the authority of government; this will shall be expressed in periodic and genuine elections which shall be by universal and equal suffrage and shall be held by secret vote or by equivalent free voting procedures.

Article 22. Everyone, as a member of society, has the right to social security and is entitled to realization, through national effort and international cooperation and in accordance with the organization and resources of each State, of the economic, social and cultural rights indispensable for his dignity and the free development of his personality.

Article 23. (1) Everyone has the right to work, to free choice of employment, to just and favourable conditions of work and to protection against unemployment.

(2) Everyone, without any discrimination, has the right to equal pay for equal work.

(3) Everyone who works has the right to just and favourable remuneration ensuring for himself and his family an

existence worthy of human dignity, and supplemented, if necessary, by other means of social protection.

(4) Everyone has the right to form and to join trade unions for the protection of his interests.

Article 24. Everyone has the right to rest and leisure, including reasonable limitation of working hours and periodic holidays with pay.

Article 25. (1) Everyone has the right to a standard of living adequate for the health and well-being of himself and of his family, including food, clothing, housing and medical care and necessary social services, and the right to security in the event of unemployment, sickness, disability, widowhood, old age or other lack of livelihood in circumstances beyond his control.

(2) Motherhood and childhood are entitled to special care and assistance. All children, whether born in or out of wedlock, shall enjoy the same social protection.

Article 26. (1) Everyone has the right to education. Education shall be free, at least in the elementary and fundamental stages. Elementary education shall be compulsory. Technical and professional education shall be made generally available and higher education shall be equally accessible to all on the basis of merit.

(2) Education shall be directed to the full development of the human personality and to the strengthening of respect for human rights and fundamental freedoms. It shall promote understanding, tolerance and friendship among all nations, racial or religious groups, and shall further the activities of the United Nations for the maintenance of peace.

(3) Parents have a prior right to choose the kind of education that shall be given to their children.

Article 27. (1) Everyone has the right freely to participate in the cultural life of the community, to enjoy the arts and to share in scientific advancement and its benefits.

(2) Everyone has the right to the protection of the moral and material interests resulting from any scientific, literary or artistic production of which he is the author.

Article 28. Everyone is entitled to a social and international order in which the rights and freedoms set forth in this Declaration can be fully realized.

Article 29. (1) Everyone has duties to the community in

which alone the free and full development of his personality is possible.

(2) In the exercise of his rights and freedoms, everyone shall be subject only to such limitations as are determined by law solely for the purpose of securing due recognition and respect for the rights and freedoms of others and of meeting the just requirements of morality, public order and the general welfare in a democratic society.

(3) These rights and freedoms may in no case be exercised contrary to the purposes and principles of the United Nations.

Article 30. Nothing in this Declaration may be interpreted as implying for any State, group or person any right to engage in any activity or to perform any act aimed at the destruction of any of the rights and freedoms set forth herein.